Dreams to Destiny

He Holds Your Hand through Every Transition in Life

Debbie Joy Mora

WestBow
PRESS
A DIVISION OF THOMAS NELSON

WestBow Press books may be ordered through booksellers or by contacting:

WestBow Press
A Division of Thomas Nelson
1663 Liberty Drive
Bloomington, IN 47403
www.westbowpress.com
1-(866) 928-1240

Because of the dynamic nature of the Internet, any Web addresses or
links contained in this book may have changed since publication and
may no longer be valid. The views expressed in this work are solely those
of the author and do not necessarily reflect the views of the publisher,
and the publisher hereby disclaims any responsibility for them.

Any people depicted in stock imagery provided by Thinkstock are models,
and such images are being used for illustrative purposes only.

Certain stock imagery © Thinkstock.

ISBN: 978-1-4497-1026-2 (sc)
ISBN: 978-1-4497-1025-5 (e)

Library of Congress Control Number: 2010943390

Printed in the United States of America

WestBow Press rev. date: 02/04/2011

Dedication

I would like to dedicate this book to my three sons, Arty, Andy and Aaron, who I am so proud of. Thank you for faithfully supporting me in my writing endeavors, knowing that God has chosen us as His vessels to fulfill our destiny in life. Although challenging struggles can be overwhelming in life's journey, it is because of my relationship with God that my life has been strengthened by His infinite love to become who I am today. Words cannot express my appreciation to my parents, who passed on such a great spiritual inheritance. I in turn, am committed to pass on to my sons the biblical principles of truth found in God's Word. My prayers are that they embrace this spiritual treasure and live their lives according to God's will. Thank you Delia Mora, my wonderful mother, who has been a living example of a true woman of God, preaching His Word around the world, impacting lives for His glory and living a holy life that is pleasing in the sight of God. Special thanks to my brother Jim and my sister Dinah, who have given countless hours of encouragement and wisdom during my seasons of transition in life. Thanks for believing with me that God's best is yet to come.

I want to express my thanks to two very special friends who have given me prayer support and inspiration to move forward to what God has in store for me. Thank you, Rhode for a lifetime of friendship and for your excellent work in editing the Spanish translation for <u>Dreams to Destiny</u>. Thank you Sister Ninfa for your friendship and support that is dear to my heart. To both of you I will forever be grateful and give thanks unto God for your lives. Truly He has placed you in my path as divine connections in my life!

I want to give all honor and glory to God, for giving me the opportunity to serve Him and for Jesus, my Savior, who has allowed me to experience such a great salvation and abounding grace. Thank you Holy Spirit for being my Teacher and Guide and for the revelation of God's power to transform lives into Your image. Thank you God for the privilege of holding my hand as I transition from my Dreams to Destiny!

Contents

Chapter 1:
Dream until you Reach your Destiny

*Become All You can Become One Day at a Time

I'll never forget how difficult it was to make my decision to let go of my dream. All little girls dream of marrying their knight in shining armor who will protect them and together share a lifetime of dreams. In 1981, my wish came true when I married the man of my dreams. At that time, I was a missionary teacher in Guatemala, Central America. When I returned home after two years oversees, I visited a church in Nogales, Arizona where I met my husband to be. After one year, I had a dream that I considered to be a confirmation from the Lord that this man was to be my husband. In that dream, we were speaking at a church meeting one Sunday morning. I was by his side, interpreting in English, while he was preaching in Spanish. Although I had never interpreted in my life, I felt it was a picture of our future ministry. So, I married my knight in shining armor and felt blessed to help my husband receive an open door for ministry, first as a missionary and later as a pastor. We were blessed as newlyweds and I was extremely happy

1

to have the opportunity to compliment my husband's ministry. We visited many churches before our missionary trip to Honduras, Central America, where we ministered at the Bible School and the churches, training leaders. We returned to the States to give birth to our first son and began to pastor in California. I thought that my marriage was divorce proof because I was doing more for the well being of my husband, making "*good deposits*" into our marriage. Nevertheless, I wasn't aware that shortly after the wedding and after a short time in ministry together, my dreams would begin to shatter, having to begin the process of letting go of my dream and allowing God to begin to guide me on a new road to my destiny!

It was the fall of 1997, and by that time we had three sons. After several months of marital counseling sessions, not one experience of change or improvement was evident on the part of my spouse. My hope for the miraculous began to fade because his arrogant character, as I knew it, had not changed and he didn't demonstrate the desire to save our marriage. Due to my desperation, I sought counsel from our denomination and knowing we were pastors, the counselor advised me to make an appointment with an attorney, due to the seriousness of the matter regarding finances, women and other factors that demonstrated evidence that the marital covenant had been broken. Although I had endured an abusive relationship, both mental and verbal for sixteen years, all my praying and having faith in the restoration of my marriage was far beyond reach because of strong pride in his life. I could not bear the thought of living like this the rest of my life without some kind of change. It takes both parties involved to desire to make it work and commit to developing a trust relationship that could once again build unity and harmony for years to come.

Malachi 2:14 talks about ..."*the wife by covenant*". According to God's unchanging purpose, marriage is a covenant, which is the secret that ensures the success of the marriage relationship. Once this secret is ignored or forgotten, marriage loses its sanctity, and therefore loses its strength and stability. A Christian marriage will not work without the supernatural grace of God and this grace is received only as husband and wife yield themselves to God and one another in covenant commitment. Without covenant, there can be no union and without commitment, there can be no covenant.

After many years of prayer, meditation and fasting on what was God's will, especially with the circumstances at a climax, I had two options.

1. I could stay in the abusive relationship, not knowing what would happen to me or my children. I knew this was not a healthy way to live, much less was it God's will.

2. I could separate myself form the abuse and trust God to be my husband and a Father to my three sons.

In order to make the right decision, I had to trust God for His grace to guide me in the decision making process and get me through what was going to change the course of my life.

I Tim. 1:14 says,

> *"The grace of our Lord was poured out on me abundantly."*

I didn't know it at the time, but His grace was about to abound on my life as never before! There are times when

God's love for us demands that He move in ways we do not understand as mentioned in …

Isa. 55:8-9:

> *"For my thoughts are not your thoughts, neither are your ways my ways, declares the Lord. As the heavens are higher than the earth, so are my ways higher than your ways and my thoughts than your thoughts."*

The reason why I accepted the counselor's suggestion to consult an attorney was because I was trying to keep my dream alive. I thought that when my husband saw the legal documents, he would think again concerning what was happening to our marriage and our sacred vows that were being severed. I thought, *"This will be his opportunity to communicate with me, demonstrate his interest and fight for his marriage."* I was so wrong! To my surprise, he accepted the court documents and responded immediately in writing that he wanted the divorce. That was the evidence that he had no interest in saving our marriage, therefore, it didn't matter if he lost it! I was shocked at his response! Nevertheless, I continued to pray that perhaps sometime throughout the process, he would reconsider his decision and open his eyes in order to think about the loss of his wife and three sons as a family. Surely, he knew that this was not the will of God; nevertheless, the opposite of God's will began to take place. Because of his ungodly attitude, he demonstrated that he wanted this to happen and only continued to stay married to me due to other personal interests. He was waiting for me to take the first step. One of his interests was that the denomination would not take his ministerial credential, which was his opportunity to pastor with the denomination and have a salary. Unfortunately, the divorce process began to take its course.

Until this day, I cannot understand how a Christian denomination has a regulation in their bylaws, placing the fault on the first one that files for divorce, not looking at the reasons why that person filed in the first place. It seems to me there should be a procedure for investigating about the marital problems in the pastor's home with reconciliation as the final goal. I began to feel a sense of disorientation. My soul felt fragmented, my spirit broken and my body reflected the pain of the situation.

Although I am not disclosing all of the details, legal matters were apparent in regards to the loss of my house and my retirement, which the law of the land calls "*community property*", which was to be divided between the both of us. He received most of the resources as he was awarded half of my retirement. He did not have any form of retirement. Because of my job, he didn't have to pay alimony and very little child support. I had to start over and was fearful and anxious about my future and the future of my sons. I had to depend on God and His power to intervene with His voice to re-create circumstances for my future.

I grew up in a Christian home and my parents were pastors. I remember many decades earlier that certain "*problems or sins*" were never spoken of from the pulpit and seldom discussed among the Christian community. A family member would identify an issue such as child abuse or adultery, and instead of taking steps to resolve the issue, they became passive, buried their feelings and avoided facing the issue all because of ministry. Some of the reasons behind their decisions of passivity are that God hates divorce and it is not God's will for a couple that God has united to end up in separation and finally divorce. So the women kept quiet and continued in their silent pain. Another reason why things were kept quiet was because of the church, the

5

scandal it would cause and how it would hurt the brethren. In the end, due to the unbearable circumstances, separation took place anyway. What was not taken into consideration at the church and denomination level was a deeper study of divorce in the Bible and why divorce was allowed. The following spiritual laws concerning marriage, adultery and divorce are mentioned in the Bible:

*The Word of God & Divorce

Matt. 5:31-32	Matrimonial Infidelity
Deut. 24:1-4	Old Testament Laws
Mark 10:2-12	Hardened Hearts
Ezra 3:1	Divorce & Adultery
Luke 16:18	Adultery
I Cor. 7:10-11	Marriage

The scriptures clearly state that our body is the temple of the Holy Spirit and the man's duty is to love his wife as Christ loves the Church. No one has the right to abuse anyone, child of God or not. Many victims keep silent, especially if they're from a pastor's home. I was willing to continue to suffer for the same reasons that other Christian leaders had suffered, due to traditional religious thinking. But I couldn't let excuses confine me in my pain or the pain of my children. Thank God it was a different generation and the present laws were written to protect families and spouses in domestic hardships. The churches are speaking more openly about the struggles in the homes, including those in ministry, although we are still not totally open. I developed the attitude, as difficult as it was, to do whatever it took to recover my life back. I began to understand my past and how the enemy was continuing to have his way because the women would not allow a scandal to take place because of ministry. All of the people involved in some form of family dysfunction had multiple scars that could not be removed because they last a lifetime. I didn't want lasting scars for my children, so I had to allow courage to stir up in my soul to take a stand for myself and my children in order for us to have a better life.

Over a decade has passed, and I'm so glad to announce that although I've been able to accomplish goals I never dreamed of, every day I am getting closer and closer to my destiny! God will do the same for you!

You are destined to be blessed!

Destiny is God's planned order of events for your future. Dreaming is important as it allows you to set goals, make plans to reach your dreams, and implement strategies to one day step into your dream. God not only has plans for you, but because He designed them, He knows the outcome which includes prosperity for every area of your life.

I Thess. 5:23 tells us:

> *"…I pray God your whole spirit and soul and body be preserved blameless unto the coming of our Lord Jesus Christ."*

The best that God has planned for you is yet to come. The choice is yours to visualize how fast you want to reach your destiny. We have to make the right decision, and in order to do that, we have to choose *"right thinking"*. After we've decided to be like-minded with God, then we will need to choose and to continue to choose right thoughts. God has placed before His people the option to choose life or death.

> *"I call heaven and earth to witness this day against you, that I have set before you life and death, the blessings and the curses; therefore, choose life, that you and your descendants may live." Deut. 30:19*

Proverbs 18:21 tells us:

> *"Death and life are in the power of the tongue, and they who indulge in it shall eat the fruit of it…"*

Our thoughts become our words because we speak what we are feeling in our heart. *"From the abundance of the heart, the mouth speaks" (Matt. 12:34)*. So, it is vitally important to choose life-generating thoughts. Then we will speak according to our thoughts of life, which are guided by the Word of God. It takes discipline and an ongoing focus on developing our mind and heart to watch what we say and pray continually. So, I encourage you to begin to discipline yourself! As we do this on a daily basis, little by little, submitting our mind to the Lord, we begin to change our thinking and our speech to be in line with God's plan for our life. Make a quality decision to renew your mind, no matter how long it takes. Work on choosing your thoughts carefully. Don't give up! You'll soon be on your way to your destiny!

When the love and trust in my marriage was being crushed by the enemy's plans, I couldn't see any kind of destiny in sight. Everything seemed dim and dark. I thought my destiny was to live with this man the rest of my life as his wife and minister together as God directed our lives. I thought it was a lifetime commitment *"until death do us part"* and my God-given assignment here on earth. But I soon found out, that I could not force him to love me or to desire to spend the rest of his life with me. Many questions began to take place in my mind. *"Could there exist another destiny for me?"* And if so, *"What kind of destiny would it be? Does God have second plans? Are they just as divine as the first?"* As confusion tried to set in, God spoke to me about the story of Joseph in the Old Testament and his experiences of betrayal, abandonment, false accusations and injustices.

From the Pit to the Prison to the Palace

When you have been placed in the pit by someone that you love, like Joseph was, you will experience betrayal, abandonment, confusion, and loneliness. As a pastor's wife, I ministered to hundreds of people, teaching the Word of God, praying for the brethren, and encouraging them, but not one was there in my time of need. The only three people that were present on a daily basis with support and prayers were my mom, my brother Jim and my sister Dinah. I also had a couple of close friends that lived out of the area that also supported me in prayer. More than anything else, I can say the grace of God was ever present to strengthen me through this difficult time in my life. Even though I didn't feel God's presence very close at times, I knew He was so near to me. His angels were ministering to my life, giving me the support I needed to get up every morning and fulfill my daily obligations of my home, my work as a teacher at school and taking care of my three sons. *II Corinthians 9:8* declares:

> *"God is able to make all grace abound to you, so that in all things at all times, having all that you need, you will abound to every good work."*

When you're placed in a prison like Joseph was, due to false accusations, you need God's wisdom and understanding to know that He is in control regardless of the adverse circumstances. Speaking to my attorney in regards to the updates on the process, I was summoned to a deposition, where I was questioned by the opposing attorney. There were many allegations and false accusations, when I had been faithful, not only as a wife and mother, but at my job and in the church. I thought I knew this man whom I had lived with for sixteen years, but I no longer knew him. The church denomination, from the District office to the Headquarters offices in Springfield, Missouri showed little interest in reconciling this pastor with his wife. Your life's testimony is the strongest reputation you could present before God and man. Sooner or later the truth becomes evident to all. In the meantime, you know your own daily walk and so does God. What matters is what God is thinking of me, not what man is thinking.

Looking at similarities between my situation and that of Joseph, we trusted God in the midst of all adversity. God continued to use his life in the area of dreams. He was gifted in interpreting dreams. Remember he was a dreamer. You must never stop dreaming because that's how you elevate your faith for your future. Declare that your life is in His hands and you will move in God's favor whether you see it or not. Joseph's betrayal and prison experience was necessary to geographically relocate him to his place of destiny, and it also conditioned him to rule. God's timing is different than our timing, but be assured that He is working out His divine plan for your life because your "*Suddenly*" awaits you.

When your "*suddenly*" manifests and comes to pass and it will, just like Joseph, in one day, you'll be in your palace. The palace represents the place that God has designed for you to be, where He will use you for His glory. Joseph was given a high government position. He was a minister in the marketplace and God used his life to save the lives of thousands during a time of famine in the land. Not only did he save many people's lives in Egypt where God had taken him, but he saved many lives in the surrounding countries, where there was lack of food due to the drought. That place that He has designed for you is the place that only you can fulfill in His plan. Sometimes we don't like the journey we have to go through to get to that place; nevertheless, there are necessary steps to get us to our destiny. It's actually a spiritual war of faith, a battle to win your family's blessings and inheritance in Christ Jesus. But, your faith in His promises will take you to a place of prosperity, power and position in the Kingdom. By considering the characteristics of God, you will realize that your heavenly Father has access to every moment in your life from the beginning to the end, just like He designed Joseph's life. Joseph fulfilled God's plan for his generation and saved an entire nation. God has a wonderful plan for you too!

God's Master Plan for You

God's master plan for you includes the following:

1. God's Plan

Your purpose depends on God's plan for your life. If He desires to place you in a particular field, it's because He has a purpose to use you in that capacity. You will be used to touch many lives for His glory!

> *Jer. 29:11* says:

> *"For I know the plans I have for you, declares the Lord, plans to prosper you and not to harm you, plans to give you hope and a future."*

2. God's Purpose

Your potential depends on God's purpose for your life. If His plan is to use you in a certain profession, He will equip you for your purpose. He will give you the ability and potential needed to fulfill that purpose. *Eph. 1:11* states:

> *"In him we were also chosen, having been predestined according to the plan of him who works out everything in conformity with the purpose of his will."*

Detours and delays don't change God's purpose for you. God's power is at work within you. If you enter a potter's house and want to know the purpose of the vessel he is forming, you don't ask the vessel do you? No! You ask the Master Potter.

3. **God's Process**

The molding process depends on God's purpose, which determines your potential. Once you discover the purpose that God has for you, you can discover the potential that He will equip you with. Don't ask, *"Can God use me in this way?"* The purpose of the vessel determines the potential of the vessel. You were called to be a vessel of honor.

II Cor. 3:5-6 declares:

> ***"Not that we are competent in ourselves to claim anything for ourselves, but our competence comes from God. He has made us competent as a minister of a new covenant – not of the letter, but of the Spirit; for the letter kills, but the Spirit gives life."***

You have the potential of touching others because of God's purpose for your life.

4. **God's Promise**

The promise to fulfill your purpose is assured from the One who planned your purpose. Opinions, suggestions, and recommendations from others besides the Creator, who established your purpose, do not cancel your purpose and potential. God just wants you to be faithful and He will do the rest through the work of the Holy Spirit. He has promised to complete the work He began in you.

Before you were in your mother's womb, God already had a plan for you, your children, and your children's children. Whatever you sow, you will reap. Sow words of faith for you and your children and you'll see His plan come to pass for you and for them. His plan is manifested from the "**written word**" to the "**spoken word**". What God has stated in

His Word needs to be transferred or manifested by you through your faith in Him because He is the Word of Life. *Mark 11:23-24* declares:

> *"... if you don't doubt in your heart but believe what you say will happen, it will be done for you. Therefore I tell you, whatever you ask for in prayer, believe that you have received it, and it will be yours."*

Your Dream will Come to Pass

Your dream will come to pass by...

1. *Accepting the challenge to believe that what you speak about your dream will come to pass.*

*We are to face our task in the power of the Holy Spirit, not in our own human strength. We know in our heart that it's by the power of the Holy Spirit that we have what we say and believe it will come to pass in the name of the Lord. Allow Him to work in you and in His timing. Don't try to help Him because that will only cause delays. Satan will try to distract you from your destiny. Don't allow him to get his way! Press in during those times of weakness, persevere with faith, trust God and rest in Him. Allow God to fight your battles. You must wait for the manifestation of the life of God in your spirit; allowing the Holy Spirit to energize and elevate your natural strength, to position you in preparation for your destiny.

2. *Yielding your will to His process in fulfilling your dream.*

* In order for your dream to come to pass, you need to be willing to submit or surrender to God as your highest authority. Your vessel needs to be prepared to take the necessary steps for your destiny, ready for the Master's use. For this to occur, a state of holiness is required and God will take the necessary time to mold your life as He prepares the clay and forms it into the beautiful vessel He so desires to use.

3. *Obeying and taking the necessary steps of faith for your dream to become your destiny.*

*Your walk on the pathway of obedience is the highest level of praise. If you are willing to obey God and willing to activate your faith to believe that God has a better future for you, know for a fact that the best days of your life are ahead of you.

Although you might not sense grace and favor over your life, let me assure you that favor and grace are upon you during your times of distress and affliction. How do I know? Others without the favor and grace of God ended up in a mental institute, committed suicide or some other tragic experience. Don't allow favor to be stripped from you by the enemy. When questions like *"What if I had done this or that?"* or *"Perhaps I should have listened to…and done this"* come to your mind, don't spend your time feeding or nurturing those thoughts.

Cindy Jacobs, in her book, <u>Women of Destiny,</u> identified five major strongholds that she had to deal with in order to be released into her destiny.[1]

1. <u>The Stronghold of the Mind</u>

   *This stronghold consists of thoughts of hopelessness that causes the believer to accept as unchangeable, situations that we know are contrary to the will of God.[2]

2. <u>The Stronghold of Fear</u>

   *This stronghold is a distressing emotion of anxiety one experiences when one is afraid of someone or something due to the challenges in life, but is contrary to the promises of God.

3. The Stronghold of Intimidation
    *This stronghold is an emotion of fear, reservation and shyness caused by a threat, which is contrary to Biblical principles found in the Word of God.

4. Generational Stronghold
    *This stronghold is a family behavior pattern that is passed on from one life cycle to another, but can be broken in the name of Jesus and by the power of His blood.

5. Stronghold of Tradition
    *This stronghold is a continuing pattern of cultural beliefs and cultural practices that do not line up with the blessings God has planned for your life.

Any of these strongholds will allow bitterness to be nurtured in your soul. All bitterness brings feelings of resentment, animosity, agony, distress and hostility. The only way to begin working on your dream is to begin to remove these negative feelings, by releasing them on a daily basis as you study and meditate on God's Word and take time in prayer and give them over to God. In his book, The Wisdom Commentary1, Dr. Murdock explains how you can overcome bitterness. Below are some of his suggestions...

1. Admit that you have bitterness in your heart and that it's damaging to you.

2. Surrender to the Spirit and meditate on the scriptures, preferably the Psalms of David.

Begin to set goals for your future. Never allow the root of bitterness to rob you of the success and joy you can experience! Reject all bitterness! Use your energy and faith on your destiny. Remember, your children are a vital part of your destiny and you must always persevere by looking to your future, not your past. Align up your thoughts with God's thoughts. Don't ever give up, because little by little you are changing for the better. The more you renew your mind on a daily basis, the more your life will be renewed as well. When you begin to see God's good plan for you in your thinking, you will begin to walk in it. The enemy wants to distort your identity in God, but soon you will say *"goodbye"* to failure and *"hello"* to favor.

Meditate on this scripture as you are going through your journey.

> *"And after you've suffered a little while, the God of all grace, who has called you to His eternal glory in Christ Jesus, will Himself complete and make you what you ought to be, establish and ground you securely, and strengthen, and settle you."*

> *I Pet. 5:10*

This word of the Lord was given by Chuck Pierce and was shared on his website "Glory of Zion, International:

> *"If you'll move with Me, you'll shine with Me. Move and shine! Watch Me position you! So, learn the winds of change and move with Me. You will change! I change not. But you will change! I'm extending a call from heaven to move. Move with Me. Make your turns with me. Turn with me for I am making a turn in your river. Feel the wind blow around your feet, for you've been in places where your peace*

has escaped you. If you'll receive My wind around your feet, you'll walk in peace in a new way. Let the wind circle your feet. Allow Me to lift you above that which you've cemented in. Watch the rearrangement of islands, for no longer will anyone be an island to themselves. Some will say, 'This island that I have been on has been my life and been my home'. But now you will be connected in a new way. No longer will you be independent in your expression and culture, but you will blend in a new way with Me. You will begin to look the way I have destined you to look. Heaven is meeting earth and the wind of the Spirit in you is rising up. I am here to raise you up. Press in! Press in! Now, all of a sudden, as faith arises from earth, heaven will respond with My wind. This will create Spirit action in the earth. Strongholds will fall and transformation will begin"

*I encourage you to arise, to know your God, His authority, His power and His anointing in you to become all you were destined to become.

1 Jacobs, Cindy, Women of <u>Destiny</u> (Ventura, CA; Regal Books, 1998, p.102-103)

2. Silvoso, Ed, <u>That None Should Perish</u> (Ventura, CA; Regal Books, 1994, p. 155)

Chapter 2:
The Unexpected Journey

*WHEN DEVASTATION HITS, THE DOOR OF FAITH OPENS WIDE

We choose our own destiny day by day. We start to make choices the moment we begin each new day. The success on how fast you will reach your destiny depends on your daily choices. Know that God made a choice when He decided to choose you, call you and design a place for you in this life.

Rejected, but not Forsaken

When the honeymoon is over and the journey of bonding begins as a married couple, it's like two rivers crashing together to form one single large lake. The married life requires commitment of love and faithfulness by both parties in order to have success. This kind of commitment gets you to an expected end, no matter the challenges that come your way because love and dedication are ever present. But when love and commitment begin to fade, your married life becomes challenging. When a spouse is unfaithful, it doesn't matter how much love and commitment you have, it takes both partners as husband and wife to be faithful one to another "*until death do us part*".

Cindy Jacobs, founder of "*Generals of Intercession*", *Inc.* speaks about "*spiritual adultery*". She explains that this type of adultery is when one of the spouses forms a bond with another person outside the home, in which he/she thinks more about the other person at their work or church than their own spouse. The marriage fails due to infidelity, which is not the fault of the person who has been faithful, much less the children. It is the fault of the person that was unfaithful, who by his/her own will, made the choice of getting involved in an inappropriate relationship. The guilty party doesn't want to be confronted about his unfaithfulness and is willing to lie, especially when he holds a position of Christian leadership. This spouse faces internal condemnation for his failure. Then he feels that he cannot resolve the issue. If your husband violated the covenant of faithfulness, it's not your fault and you should not be condemning yourself. If you are doing the best you can with your home as wife and mother, it's not your fault that your husband can't be man enough to control the temptations and be faithful to his marriage and his family. This was evident in my husband's behavior and the time he spent with us, his own family, as compared to the time he spent with female leaders in the church.

When I began to have my suspicions of his unfaithfulness in regards to the marital covenant, I began to notice signs of change in his behavior. It seemed like he kept secrets, avoided conversations and answers to my questions. He would lie about schedules, appointments on his calendar, and especially about arriving home very late at night on a daily basis. I thought, "*Surely, he wouldn't break his marital covenant. He's a pastor who preaches every week from the pulpit.*" Nevertheless, he totally avoided holding conversations with me. Unanswered questions continued month after month and year after year. His only answer was "*You don't understand.*" Of course, I had grown up in a pastor's home and as a pastor's daughter; I had developed discernment with certain behaviors because my dad had these similar behavior patterns. When I began to see the same behaviors in my husband, I tried speaking with him, but he only accused me of being jealous. When I questioned him about coming home late at night every day, his answer was that he had long meetings, but he was actually working with the secretary of the church, who was going through a divorce. I tried to warn him about the danger he was exposing himself to, but he never accepted my advice because "*I didn't know what I was talking about*". I could not believe this was happening to me, a believer with Christian values, totally committed to the marital covenant and a pastor's wife.

When your spouse tells you that everything is your fault, elements in a healthy relationship are off balance. It is never one person's fault for everything that happens in a marriage. Both persons are responsible and contribute to the relationship, whether good or bad. I felt excluded with his silent treatment throughout my years of marriage. Even so, hoping to maintain unity in the marriage and because I loved my husband and my children, I gave an unending effort to make sure the family stayed together, while waiting for a change in his life. But when a spouse has decided he wants out of the relationship, only God could intervene and change the hardened heart of a person. If the spouse believes he is right, even though he's wrong, he will make decisions according to his thoughts and his own will. He doesn't give place to reflect and evaluate his own behaviors and decisions. That's called pride! Even when the situation continues with no hope in sight, then it's time to seek counselors, therapists, ministers, psychologists and any other remedial help for the reconciliation of the marriage and the goal of rebuilding the relationship in order to save the marriage. But if the spouse demonstrates no change and doesn't admit his mistakes, even when he is willing to attend the counseling sessions, but believes he is right, hope for the marriage grows very dim. Reconciliation is a wonderful experience for those that are privileged enough to experience it. Only God's intervention can bring about change. But when the spouse has already made up his mind, very little can be done when he is unwilling to accept accountability. Then, devastation begins to surround the household and the door for divorce is open due to marital unfaithfulness.

It has been documented that those who cause the divorce rarely seek counseling of any kind, much less professional help. They don't believe they need it, because they don't believe they were the cause for heartache in the first place. They think they're right and don't need to search for answers by evaluating their own lives, so they seldom consult with marriage counselors. Very rarely do they assume personal responsibility for their conflicts. This was my experience!

Related to rejection are the wounds of betrayal due to broken trust. *Proverbs 15:13* tells us:

> *"A happy heart makes the face cheerful, but heartache crushes the spirit."*

In his book, Experiencing God's Power, Derek Prince states that the primary result of rejection is the inability to receive or communicate love. A person who has never experienced being loved cannot transmit love. Even if our parents didn't show us love, God doesn't desire that we suffer from their mistakes. Nor does He desire that our children suffer due to lack of love. A person that doesn't deal with rejection through God's healing power will experience loneliness, self-pity, depression and hopelessness. The final result could be tragic. Others react to rejection with resentment, hatred and finally rebellion. It would bring more devastation to go down that route, so one must stay focused on inner healing. *I Sam. 15:23* tells us that *"…rebellion is as the sin of witchcraft"*. By accepting God's provision, you can cut off that rejection once and for all. When you begin to sense healing of this wound of rejection is when you make a prayer for your former spouse and ask God to bless him. It seems like the most unnatural thing to do, but then God is supernatural.

After much thought on the family history and the study of the Word of God, according to the pattern of behavior in the lives of the men in my family, there was a cycle of sin from generation to generation in which the men affected the course of history because it radically changed our lives as wives and children forever. Rejection caused by a broken relationship is a curse. *Malachi 4:5-6* tells us…

> *"I will send you the prophet Elijah before that great and dreadful day of the Lord comes. He will turn the hearts of the fathers to their children, and the hearts of the children to their fathers; or else I will come and strike the land with a curse."*

But *Eph. 1:6* so wonderfully explains *"He has made us accepted in the Beloved"*, which means *"highly favored one"*.

One of the most damaging effects on a family is separation and divorce. It's not only the separation of man and woman; it's the tearing apart of what was once joined together.

Broken homes leave a trail of broken dreams, emotionally damaged people and children, broken and traumatized for the rest of their lives. But, your past does not necessarily dictate the outcome of your future. After you realize this truth, then follows the process of releasing the hurt. God has been faithful and most of the adult children in my family that have experienced domestic hardship are serving the Lord, but we have all been affected by the behaviors of those who came before us.

One of the greatest areas that have impacted our lives is shame. This traumatic experience reshapes a person's life in ways that one doesn't realize. People are thoroughly different after a traumatic experience because as a survivor, you become more cautious, often less trusting and more aware of your immediate environment. Values such as safety and attachment become more important and you are on the alert to notice these factors in the present and future. There's so much healing that needs to take place and with God's help, you will use your experience to help others.

As I researched about some of the problems why people in ministry tend to fail, I found out that some of the common reasons are the following…

1. Hidden or repressed anger, often involving unresolved conflicts from the past

2. Ongoing living in the fast lane (Burnout)
    *Constantly being on the go with church activities can cause great exhaustion if you don't take a break from everything once in awhile and spend time with your family.

3. The superstar syndrome (Pulpit ministry with ongoing flattering words of admiration from others)

4.   Working without being accountable

Research has shown that when a person doesn't deal constructively with his anger, he will distance himself from his wife and family looking for emotional support outside of the home.[1] As a result, he will probably seek emotional support outside his marriage. Then, it won't be long until temptation overtakes him. When men fall into this trap, all the people around him suffer the consequences. Research has also found that emotional deficits and low self-esteem from childhood are major contributing factors when someone has an affair.[2] Any leader, male or female, can thrive on the praise of others and become heroes to their admirers. Whenever the family needs the pastor, he is not there for them, but he's there for the brethren. Everyone, even pastors and their wives, needs a personal support system, which should be the family, but if he's never home, how can the family give him the support he needs?

Our hearts are often out of line with God's Word and we make choices daily without consulting God's Word for wisdom on our decisions. We can either deny our behavior, continue to behave the way we do with our attitude, or decide it's not pleasing to God and choose to change. Denying our ungodly attitude is simply keeping it unspoken and saying we'll pretend it just isn't there. We need to try to uphold our standards and begin to see the plan of God for our life.

When feeling utter distress and helpless, that's the time to do what David did in *I Samuel 30*. He strengthened himself in God. During these times of turmoil, when you feel confused, depressed and anxious, you have two options:

A.   You can sink into despair and depression

B. You can strengthen yourself in God

How can I strengthen myself when I have no strength at all?

There are two steps to take during your yielding process:

1. *Wait upon God*

   Isaiah 40:29-31 says:

   "He gives strength to the weary and increases the power of the weak. Even youth grow tired and weary, and young men stumble and fall; but those who hope in the Lord will renew their strength. They will soar on wings like eagles; they will run and not grow weary, they will walk and not faint."

It took time for me to decide to make a change from those events that I had no control over. I found the potential of my future because of His wonderful power operating in my life. It took time for God to mold me again to be the "*me*" He wanted me to be. Wait upon Him and be patient with His timing for His timing is perfect and everything will align according to His perfect will. He is working on your behalf. *Isaiah 30:18* will bring you much hope.

> *"And therefore the Lord waits looking and longing to be gracious to you; and therefore He lifts Himself up, that He may have mercy on you and show loving kindness to you. For the Lord is a God of justice. Blessed are all those who wait for Him, who expect and look and long for Him."*

2. *Trust in the Lord*

Prov. 3:5-6 says:

"Trust in the Lord with all your heart and lean not unto your own understanding. In all your ways acknowledge Him and He shall direct your paths."

You are not responsible for the horrible events that happened in your past. No one goes though life without some wounding of the heart. Oftentimes we're unaware of the extent of the damage to our hearts until we're in difficult situations and our bitterness reveals itself in our words and actions. God is a God that forgives, heals and restores. We need to trust Him as He works on placing all of the pieces of the puzzle into place for us.

Divine Connections are around the Corner

The pain of the reality that separation and divorce is actually taking place in your family seems to bring you destruction for a lifetime and the life of your family members. You feel that everything is over. But, the support of family and friends is something that has no price on the value of moving forward one day at a time. Thank God for family and friends with a compassionate heart, willing to minister to those they love. I have no words that can express my gratefulness to my mom, my brother Jim and my sister Dinah who have given me endless hours of encouragement and support during my trying times and continue to do so even in the present. A couple of close friends that I've known for many years have given me ongoing support as well. God also used people that I didn't know, who brought that word of encouragement I needed. Just getting that phone call, word of encouragement, going out for a cup of coffee, a simple prayer, or a card in the mail through this difficult time brings hope into one's life. You go through a sense of "*no destiny*", especially when you thought your marriage would be a lifetime relationship and nothing else ever crossed your mind.

In the middle of change comes loneliness. I don't mean the loss of affection, but the loss of direction. You have to begin to live where you are. It's going to take your most determined effort to stop reliving "*yesterday*". Satan wants to destroy your progress of the present by tempting you with concentrating thoughts on the past. You have to get involved with "*present*" opportunities. Although times of loneliness are more apparent when the children are not present, it's an opportunity to spend time with God, surrender everything to Him and seek His guidance. I remember going through what seemed like an emotional roller coaster. My vessel felt empty, but I didn't realize that my "*emptiness*" was preparing me for whatever God wanted to " *fill* " me with. I was so glad I had my three sons and family to love, because that's what kept me going; my love for them.

But, as difficult as the pain of rejection, betrayal, and shame your experience is, there are connections and encounters with others that will come into your life within the following weeks, months and even years that will encourage you to move forward and help you reach your new destiny. You need a burning desire for the future, the kind of desire that overcomes past fear. You will remain chained to your past and all the secrets therein until you decide: Enough is enough! At that point, you break out of prison. If you're in this situation in your life, I encourage you to sense a spiritual earthquake coming your way. Just begin to praise in the middle of the midnight hours. The angels of heaven are ready to approach your circumstances, break your chains off and set you free. Hallelujah!

When God is ending one season and beginning another, or taking us through transition, He has to end or bring to death some old situations, like an abusive relationship, because He has something better for His chosen vessel. While exercising my faith, waiting for God's intervention to change the man's life and while I did whatever was possible to maintain the unity in the family, counselors said the children were not going to be happy or at ease living in a divided home. How long would it take to see change? The fact is there was evidence of unfaithfulness and the marital covenant had been broken. Although the most difficult decision in my life was to make a change and seek legal help, it was my first step towards my healthy future. As painful as it was to walk into a lawyer's office to file for divorce, it was more devastating to receive his response of wanting a divorce. I had tried everything possible and I didn't know what else to do. I thought when he received the divorce papers; he would reconsider his decision and try to resolve the problems in order to rescue his marriage. I imagined him coming to me with the desire of communicating because he didn't want to lose his marriage or his children.

But, it was just my imagination, trying to think and speak those things that were not as though they were. I was doing all I could to use my faith, speaking positive things about my marriage according to the Word of God. But by this time, my emotional upset didn't allow me to stand firm due to his constant rejection. He had preached so many years, but never fought for his marriage, not once. His silent treatment continued even after he was served with the court papers. He silence spoke louder than words. He was still living at home although he did not fulfill any financial obligations. He didn't even approach me about my decision nor had the decency of explaining his decision either. He didn't try talking to me about working it out because he wanted a divorce. He didn't want to be the first one to make the move because he wanted to blame me and use it as an explanation to the church and the denomination. He was waiting for me to make the first move. I would have waited as long as it took to reconcile, but he was pushing me further away from him, not only at home, but at church as well. I was an active pastor's wife and operated in the gifts God gave me, playing the piano, interpreting his sermons, helping at the altar with prayer, teaching Sunday school, and leading the choir just to mention some of my involvement in ministry. One Sunday morning, he replaced me with another pianist. Then, he told the congregation that I wasn't interpreting and this went on for weeks. He never asked me about it and was lying to the congregation. That Sunday morning in July, I heard the audible voice of God say to me, *"He's not rejecting you. He's rejecting me."* I never thought he would take his ungodly actions this far.

Change began to quickly take place by court dates, lawyers, and child visitation orders, not to mention the house, the bank account, assets, furniture, pictures, file documents, taxes, and so much more. I had to learn to live one day at a time, taking care of my children, going to work to support them, and beginning to take total responsibility of my household. I experienced denial for some time because it was difficult to believe this was happening to me as a pastor's wife. I believed God to work His divine miracle, not knowing that He was working it out by getting me out of that kind of controlling relationship. I had to learn to accept my reality about my own daily personal experiences in regards to no longer placing my trust in the man that I thought I would live with the rest of my life. I began to call him *"the father of my children"*. The word *"husband"* was no longer part of my vocabulary. Not even *"My ex"* was in my vocabulary because the word *"my"* represents possession and I didn't want to be associated with a man that wanted nothing to do with me any longer. He had other interests and I was no longer of any interest to him. I couldn't continue to deceive myself, thinking that he would return to become my husband. I asked my children about changing my married name back to my maiden name. Because they saw their dad's improper behavior, they agreed and supported my decision. I needed to get my life back to what it was before I married him. I was finally on the road to recovery.

<u>Vision for a New Beginning</u>

In today's world, it seems we've been overchallenged and underenabled. But, let me assure you that there is *"One"* that will enable you to take your challenges head on. He will equip you even in those times when you have no more strength to believe, to endure, to work, or even to stand firm. In the same way that the Holy Spirit of God equips you with intellectual abilities and spiritual capacities, He will equip you with emotional strength through your journey during times of challenges. In fact, the more responsibility you have before you, the more enablement or empowerment He gives you in order to carry it out.

How do I get through this journey of change? I need to submit my *"Attitudes"* and my *"Actions"* to God. I need to pray, *"I surrender all of me to your authority, Lord Jesus."* Pray that He would enlighten you to receive new insight, to see things clearly during this time of confusion, when you don't know exactly which way to turn. This is your time to trust Him who is able to complete the work that He began in you. The power of the Holy Spirit will rest upon you, open your eyes in order to see His will, quicken your soul to feel His presence when you feel all alone, and strengthen your heart, having done all, to stand firm, and strengthen your hands to continue to labor and achieve for yourself and your children. God is so good!

You are a vessel made by God's hands and even through this process of divorce, He is molding you to become all you can become in Him. Sometimes your vessel feels empty, useless, ineffective and worthless. Your thoughts are shaken with everything that is going around you. It's difficult to mediate on God's Word and His plan for your life. Your mind is bombarded with thoughts like, *"He said…"* and *"The brethren said…"* Your destiny seems to have disappeared, ceased to exist and passed suddenly from sight. But God speaks of you differently. You need to meditate on what He says about you. This is the time to conquer your goal by allowing God in His timing to successfully complete His plan in your life. When those feelings arise within you, don't just make goals to make it through the day. Take advantage of everything that God has for you, even when you don't feel like using your faith and believing in Him. Speak to your body, soul and spirit. This is the time to activate your faith. Visualize what God has planned for you, even though you don't know what that might be. Just see your life whole again. The vision that God has for you must give birth in your spirit. You can be a vessel of commitment and faith. A vessel of commitment without faith is limited. A vessel of faith without commitment is limited. But a vessel of faith with commitment is unlimited.

Think of the word **VISION** in the following terms:

V – *Vow* to God and to your children

I - *Invest* in yourself and your children

S – *Serve* God and your children

I – *Impart* to your children and others

O – *Obey* God and His Word

N – *Nourish* your relationship with God and your children

Until you have a vision to move forward, you will always live in struggles of *"yesterday"*. This is why it's necessary to speak to your emotions and stir up that desire to move forward. The desire for your new future has got to be greater than the memories of the past pain. When the desire to move forward with passion comes back into your spirit, it will begin to release you from the pain. There will be times of great stretching when you want to give up and lay aside the vision for your future. Without vision, we can't see the provision God has made available to us. If we can't see the provision, our supply for the future will be easily cut off by the enemy. Whatever you do, decide to serve the Lord in the midst of injustices, tragedies and adverse circumstances. Sometimes you'll experience feelings of inferiority, loneliness and weariness, but look to God at that moment of frustration and turn all confusion over to Him. You'll experience thoughts of rejection, disappointment and hopelessness in the deepest part of your soul, but allow God to embrace you with His eternal love. Even though fear, insecurity and discouragement are felt in the pit of your stomach, come against all inadequacy and distress that wants to make a place in your heart and when your strength fails, know that God will fight on your behalf. Don't allow unforgiveness and anger sleep with you at night, for you will not sleep well. Instead, allow the Holy Spirit to be in charge and let Him take all your burdens. These are feelings that the enemy will use against you to give up on your destiny. Satan will try to devour your finances, the harmony in your home, and your peace of mind. You can become so bound by worry over your finances and the fear of losing them, that it can keep you from doing the things God wants you to do and being the person God wants you to be. Know that your supply existed before you ever had a need. His supply is adequate for everything that you will encounter from now until eternity. Understand it well! God is your Provider! You have to learn to place all of these feelings of lack and inadequacy on the altar for God to consume with His fire and love.

Words that have been spoken over you can also cause distress. These words that have been shared between persons, good or bad, can stay in one's memory and in one's heart for a lifetime. Those inappropriate, offensive words that came at you must also be placed at the altar of God and left there. Remember, Joseph told his brothers that although they had meant their actions for evil, God meant it for good. It took years before God's plan came to pass, but nevertheless, Joseph waited on God and at the appointed time stepped into his destiny.

Exchange the Old for the New

During times of great change and transition, you must allow the Lord to redirect your focus and your steps. It's time to let go of the old in order to embrace the new. You can't receive what God wants for your life by looking back. In the midst of every obstacle, mountain, or wall that attempts to block your progress, the Lord forms a way of escape and an opportunity for breakthrough with a new beginning. "*Yesterday*" is behind us. "*Yesterday*" cannot dictate what your "*tomorrow*" will hold. Sometimes God takes His time when bringing us our full deliverance. He uses the difficult periods of waiting to stretch our faith and to let patience have her perfect work.

James 1:4 declares:

> **"Perseverance must finish its work so that you may be mature and complete, not lacking anything."**

God's timing is perfect. He is never late. So, wake up to the new possibilities that are being offered. We need to have the attitude that God is working, no matter what we may feel or how the situation may look. Sometimes in our desperate struggles, we shrink back or hide in caves of despair or depression. Believe in God's Word and release your faith, confessing victory. This will help you establish a new way of thinking, walking and talking on your journey towards your destiny. Learn to enjoy where we are while walking on our journey to our destiny. The wrong attitude will not get us there any faster. So, speak to your emotions and allow God to have all the glory by your sacrifice of obedience. God alone holds your future! Place your hope and trust in Him for He knows how He will bring your future to pass!

Isaiah 43:18-19 says,

> **"Forget the former things; do not dwell on the past. See, I am doing a new thing! Now it springs up; do**

you not perceive it? I am making a way in the desert
and streams in the wasteland."

Only God can make a way where there seems to be no way. In order for God to fill your cup and allow it to overflow, you must first empty all of the negative things, hindrances and distractions of the past. Those things from the past, whether a person, event, or circumstance that hurt you, may be the source of your wrong attitude and behavior. But don't allow it to become an excuse to stay that way. God's invisible presence goes with you in your conflicts. You might not be able to see the manifested pillar of fire or the holy pillar cloud of God, but let me assure you that He is ever present. With the Lord on your side, you are assured of victory. Don't be discouraged, but be determined to reach your goal to become all He wants you to become in Him.

I was totally crushed by someone I had trusted with my life. I felt devastated and ruined. During my times of loneliness and weariness, I had to cling onto God, my only resource. I knew that with Him, my present circumstances would change. What you are willing to walk away from, determines what God will bring to you. I knew that God would rebuild me and allow me to grow in Him. I knew it would take time, but I had to invest my effort in order to start enjoying life again, loving again and learning the real secrets of inner peace through Jesus, my new Husband.

I read the following corporate prophetic word given by Eileen Fisher during her "Prophetic School of the Holy Spirit" meeting in Colorado Springs, Colorado. This Word brought comfort to my soul as I continued to walk my path of transition, looking forward to the fulfillment of God's promises in my life.

I heard the Lord say, *"I am looking for vessels that feel empty of themselves. They even feel empty of dreams, hopes, plans and purpose. For I have shaken that which could be shaken even unto the foundation of the earth. I have shaken out dreams of the soulish realm. I have shaken out visions that came from man. For I have seen hearts that have been broken over and over, and left bleeding with no understanding of why. I have counted the tears and I have felt the hearts that have been shattered to where the pieces have been tossed to and fro. For in My Word I have spoken that all things are possible with Me. So today, I would come and I would rest My hand upon your head, and My other hand I would place upon your heart, and I would command the wind of change to come. For have I not said in My Word I have come to heal the brokenhearted, to set the captives free, to proclaim liberty? I have come to take your spirit and set it free; I have come to heal your heart, that it could not only give love, but receive love. Have you not remembered in My Word that God is love? Let My love flow and receive it into your heart. Receive it just as you received salvation in faith. Believe it! Reach out for it! Go beyond your understanding, come into the Spirit and let My Spirit exchange disappointment today. For I want to take off of you disappointment and place upon you divine appointments. For I want to rearrange your schedules. I want to rearrange your plans, your vision, and your purpose. I want to even recall your callings. I want to place you at a higher level. I would not allow you to suffer in the soulish realm when I have grace and the anointing to cause you to rise up into the spiritual realm. For My grace I would place upon your feet. You will not lose ground, but you will claim ground, ground that has been robbed and stolen. For I am calling aside My own to be renewed and refreshed. To those who are battle-fatigued, I would say, "Come off the battlefield and lay on the bridal gown". When I say this, I mean, speak to your position in Me. Pick up the armor. Put on the gown of righteousness, for when you come into that gown of righteousness, you come into who you were called to be, right-standing, right authority, right-mindedness, rightly called, and rightly positioned."*

So, get ready to become the woman you were meant to be!

1. Raymond, T. Brock and Horace C. Lukens, "Affair Prevention in the Ministry", *Journal of Psychology and Christianity* 8, no. 4 (1989): 44.

2. Steinke, <u>Clergy Affairs</u>, p. 57

Chapter 3:
The Broken Rib will Heal

*Opportunities for Greatness
come from Brokenness

The X-ray tells the Truth

I fell on the sharp corner of the table one evening in church and fractured two ribs as revealed by the x-rays in the emergency room. The doctor said he couldn't give me any treatment. I just needed to rest and take care of myself without making much movement. I had to learn how to breathe slowly because breathing deeply caused pain as the ribcage was pressed by the lungs expanding when I breathed. I had to lay still and have very limited movement for a several weeks until the healing began to take place. The doctor said it would take approximately 6-8 weeks to heal completely.

Two years later, while in another city on a ministry trip with my mom, I remembered that incident and by this time, I was already going through the process of divorce. I had this revelation about the broken rib and remembered the story in the Bible when God created Eve. He took a rib from Adam to create the woman, his helpmeet. The broken rib I had experienced represented the broken relationship between my husband and me. By this time, the physical broken rib had been healed and although during the process of healing, pain and discomfort was experienced with movement and change, it was temporary until the complete healing took place. It's taken years to heal from a broken relationship, but once I realized that healing was possible, hope began to flourish and a dream for a new destiny began to develop. I began to move again with expectancy that something good was going to happen because the worst had already passed. I had been at a standstill, but this time I began to move in a different direction; a positive direction moving forward and walking towards my destiny. Blessed be His Name!

As I studied about broken relationships, I came to realize there are some stages that a person goes through in their transition from divorce to destiny.

Stages of Transition

1. ***Denial:*** This is when we ignore or minimize what has happened to our marriage and hope that it will be taken care of. It's difficult to face the fact that "*This is happening to me*".

2. ***Anger***: You begin to fear what is going to happen next, so your defense is anger, caused by rejection.

3. ***Depression***: You feel devaluated and sad, especially around the birthdays, anniversaries, New Year's Day, Christmas and other holidays.

4. ***Acceptance:*** When you begin to see recovery, then you begin to accept the fact that there is a future for

you. There are new goals and a peace that begins to fill your heart and mind.

5. **Hope:** You begin to see that there is purpose without those involved in your past. You have a new motivation for tomorrow.

6. **Fulfillment:** During this season in your life, the" *past*" is the "*past*". You don't have to rehearse old memories because your "*future*" is now the "*present*".

I had to renew my thoughts by refocusing on my future and asking God to give me a new vision for my life. Your vision needs to be focused on the Healer, not on the sickness, on our Deliverer, not the problems, on our Victories, not the defeats, on the Power of God, not on one's weakness, on the Peace of God, not confusion, on our Faith in God, not doubt. Finally, you need to focus on Your Destiny, not the past. The Holy Spirit will help you every step of the way!

The Truth will be revealed by your Heart

You have the choice to leave the past or carry it. You have the choice to be loyal to God's plan in your life or not. You have the choice to be supportive to your children, to help them reach their destiny. What you do today will affect your children's destiny as well. My focus was on what was happening to me and I sometimes forgot what the children were going through. They were heartbroken themselves and were in a state of confusion with regards to having to adjust to having two homes, going back and forth, trying to please both mom and dad and endeavoring to do well in school at the same time.

Since their father would not talk to me, my frustration and anger allowed me to begin to evaluate how I was to deal with the children so they would get through this journey successfully. Since my actions were an expression of what was in my heart, I realized I needed to continue to surrender my all to God. During my season of grief, I had to learn to forgive one day at a time. Grief and self-pity will rob you of your strength, the very strength you need to move into a season of life that is greater than you had before the loss. Once we get wounded and experience loss due to our difficult circumstances, we can easily lose sight of God's promises. But, although during this great time of testing, when our bodies, minds and emotions tend to grow discouraged, know that His angels of grace are ministering to your life.

The biggest enemy we have to contend with is self-pity. It keeps us from seeing God's glory manifested in our life. Our *"self"* rises up and causes us to say, *"Pity me. I've lost it all. Everything's over for me."* This is the time to choose to believe that God is our Healer. We can choose to forgive or we can allow our mind-set to form self-pity. Perhaps we have a tendency to accuse God for the trauma that we are experiencing and ask Him questions like, *"Why have you allowed this to happen to me, God? I don't deserve this."* But as you look at God's Word, you will realize there are many reasons why the enemy would desire to stop God's plan for your life. The main reason is that you are a threat to the kingdom of darkness if you fulfill God's precious plan by winning souls and mentoring others that will move forward to fulfill their destiny in God. God's grace is available to help you cross the bridge to your inheritance.[1] God's purpose for you doesn't cease when you experience loss. In fact, God may have a great purpose for you within your loss. God's purpose is established in heaven, no matter the challenges that come down your path. Your life changes and so does your view of life. Things look and feel so different, that you know God is really in the middle of all that you're experiencing. Feelings of doubt and anxiety come because you don't know what lies ahead, but you must trust that God knows what can and what cannot follow you into your new season. Moving forward into the restoration God has planned depends on how you respond in the time of transition. You must ask God to reveal to you what needs to be left behind in the old season. This is vital in order to transition successfully. You will not be able to make this transition successful unless you include forgiveness.

Forgiveness is the key to a healing heart. If you don't learn to forgive, your destiny will be delayed for as long as you're ready to forgive. Shame and confusion will try to set in, but refuse to allow them to stay by continuously rejecting those feelings and meditating on who God says you are. It seems that the longer a person is a Christian, the greater the religious shame he/she carries. Shame is false guilt. It gives you the sense that "*I am inadequate and worthless as a person*". This attitude or belief is sometimes passed on from the parents to the children. Therapists call this pattern that goes from one generation to another "*multigenerational transmission*", but the Bible calls it a "*curse*". It's like a river flowing uninterrupted for generations because the behaviors continue from one generation to the next. It's my responsibility to understand the roots of that shame, to understand the experience of my own hurt and to make different choices in the present. It's up to me, with the enablement of the Holy Spirit, to stop the cycle of pain. This is done by relying on God's strength one day at a time to make wise choices. The more you understand your past, the greater the possibility you will be able to control what you will pass on to the next generation. You need to understand the problems (sins) in the family tree because you do not want the "*sins of the fathers*" to get passed down the family tree into the lives of your children. We need to declare, "*My children will be blessed*!

While reading <u>Secrets of your Family Tree</u>, I found that there are people in ministry that enter the ministry for dysfunctional reasons. People who enter the ministry are often "*people helpers*", but when they carry this gift to the point where they feel they're not ministering, unless they are always helping someone, this is a dysfunctional pattern. Some pastors and church leaders serve to the point of exhaustion and burdens with no happiness to enjoy their most precious God given gifts, their wife and family. Some feel "*manipulated*" by unreasonable demands and a slow resentment begins to build within. Below are some warning signs to look for…

- A compulsion to "*minister*" to others people's problems

- Always saying "*yes*" to others and "*no*" or "*wait*" to your family

- Doing for others what they can do for themselves

- Feeling empty if there isn't a problem to solve or someone to help

- Dropping everything because someone needs "*ministering*"

A codependent person is one who depends on satisfying the needs of others in order to feel his/her own value. So a pastor, Christian leader or any other person that follows these feelings is promoting their own dysfunction. In Christ, we can find a personal sense of value simply because we are

God's children, not because we are *"needed"* by others in the church. Those in ministry are placed on a pedestal and for those men and women of God that are not surrendering their life daily by prayer; they have a greater risk of allowing the flesh to rule. In many cases, people may be very busy with religious activities and yet be unable to make a success of their marriage. This was my case. My husband loved the attention, position and the power that went with his title. Pride can be a very dangerous characteristic that can cause you to fall if not dealt with immediately. You can't give a man any words of wisdom is he believes he's right. He wanted to counsel women alone, and although I tried to explain that this particular method of counseling was not wise, I was always *"jealous"* and *"didn't know what I was talking about"*. Of course, this was the way that he opened the door to the enemy's strategy to cause him to error. I was trying to protect my marriage from the *"appearance of evil"* with the opposite sex, but he didn't agree because his counseling sessions were a way of feeding his ego. I continued to give my faithful prayer support, knowing that he was in great danger. It was only a matter of time that something ungodly was about to develop if he didn't make lifestyle changes. I felt I didn't have the freedom to be honest and truthful about my opinions and values because they were different from his and he didn't accept or value my opinions. If I did express my opinion, I would pay some kind of consequence, usually the *"silent treatment"*. Since I wasn't able to discuss anything with him, the circumstances were controlled by his feelings, perceptions and desires. *What could I do if he thought he was right?* I felt powerless and helpless. I had no control over my life in regards to my marriage and my only resource was God. He was going to help me with whatever was going to happen because my husband's decisions were not in line with the Word of God and I knew that my children and I were going to pay the consequences someday, whatever they might be. Although my trust was in God, I just couldn't understand the road ahead and why we should have to take that route when it was not our doing. My hope for my marriage began to diminish.

Prov. 13:12 says:

> ***"Hope deferred makes the heart sick.'***

I began to feel controlled by him at a deeper level than before and my heart began to suffer because in the past, I always asked for forgiveness, although it wasn't my fault. He didn't know how to ask for forgiveness due to his pride and cultural male chauvinism. This time I had to do what was right after sixteen years and I was not going to allow him to belittle me anymore. I didn't realize that all hell was about to break loose.

His Strength during your Transition

It took two years for my transition of divorce because that's how long it took to go through the court system. The transition was not only for me, but for my three wonderful sons as well. Thank God children have a wonderful God-given mechanism called" *adjustment"* that is bestowed upon them for changes in life. Some will do well with change and others won't, depending on their character and personality. This is one of the reasons why children grow up too soon.

Since their father was not taught about respecting people's boundaries early in life, it negatively impacted our family. Even when you are taught to respect other people and their rights to express their desires, you can sometimes become confused, especially when going through your transition because of the endless questions you have in your mind.

So, during the divorce process and beyond, if you feel abandoned because your children have to visit their father due to the court order, don't convey guilt or shame messages about their lack of love and loyalty to you. I know it's not fair that the court has to have the say or control on the lives of your children and your life by setting a schedule. But, your children have the right to visit their father. It is the rule of the law and you could otherwise break the law if you don't abide and consequences could follow. When your children turn 18 years old, they can have their own schedule and will hopefully be wise to make the right choices. Some youth will still sense the need to split their time in order to please both parents, but at least the court order is lifted and so is the stress for your children. You will feel threatened by the increasing loss of control you have over your children. Don't use anger or criticism to convey your unhappiness over your being separated from them. When your children are with you and demonstrating different behaviors that are not allowed in your home, but are allowed in the other home, don't express your anger at them. Just teach them why you have your rules and with wisdom, help them feel loved. Children today will play the games necessary to please both parents. It can be a survival mechanism for some. They will try to manipulate their parents during this time as well by making the circumstances work in their favor. They might sense some competition between the parents and you must let them know that it's not a game, but help them to develop, mature and become the best they can become in God. I began to change my schedule in order to allow quality time with my sons when they were with me. Then I did all of my chores, bills, laundry, grocery and other responsibilities on the days that the boys were visiting their father. You might experience some of the following feelings within during your new steps as single again, but God is with you and you are not alone. Surrender your emotions to your Healer who is able to develop the new "*you*"!

1. Hidden anger
2. Life out of control
3. No sense of identity
4. Constantly blaming others
5. Depression
6. Anxiety

If you have the ability to go to Christian counseling or are able to get a hold of a good counseling book or CD, take advantage of those opportunities to take care of yourself. Your children need for you to be emotionally healthy and stable.

The answer for restoration is still the same; prayer and the Word of God. This is when grace comes into the picture for you. Grace is the lack of condemnation.

Romans 8:1 tells us:

> **"...there is now no condemnation for those who are in Christ Jesus."**

We need to learn to "*live*" and "*stand*" in grace. It's not by our deeds or actions that we take a righteous stand, but the opposite is true. Although we don't deserve it, God's love and mercy allows us access grace as mentioned in ***Rom.5:2***.

> **"...we have gained access by faith into this grace in which we now stand."**

People who grow up in families that deal with failure in dysfunctional ways exhibit many symptoms of dysfunction. One is, for example, the *"I'm never wrong"* attitude. This person cannot admit that he fails. He's immature, insecure and considers himself the *"savior"* of the world. You need to face the facts that he will not change until he surrenders all of his will to God. If he doesn't believe he has anything to surrender, he will not change. That means that the circumstances will not change until God intervenes. Your feelings of frustration must be calmed by surrendering them completely to God. Even when you don't feel like fighting against these feelings of frustration, press in and persevere, because if they overpower you, you won't fulfill God's purpose in your life until you overcome the thoughts of your past. This extra baggage will be heavy and it'll take you longer to reach your destiny. So, dismiss the extra weight by letting go and letting God guide you on your path to your destiny. Like God's people in the desert, you will go round and round the mountain until you obey His commandments, which are His laws in your heart. Move forward! Take steps towards your destiny! When you're walking, think to yourself, *"I'm possessing the land and territory that God is giving me for my future and the future of my children. I receive my portion in Jesus' name."* Commit yourself to excellence! Why settle for less when you can have the best? Remember, you are a woman of excellence! You are a vessel of honor!

I spent the first few years during and after the divorce with ongoing confessions of forgiveness. But when everything that had happened was going through my mind, it was hard to forgive, especially during the entire process of divorce because I had to deal with attorneys, attend the court appointments and prepare all of the paperwork. I thought about my children and how all of this was affecting them. Trying to surrender my thoughts to God, I kept busy, taking care of the house and working as teacher at my job. When I look back and reflect on those difficult times, I have come to realize that one of the functions of the power of salvation and deliverance is "*redeeming the past*" from the hand of the enemy, so it is no longer a weapon against me and my children.

The boys would come back from visiting their dad and share what was going on in the other household with people and women visiting and staying in the home on an ongoing basis. He had left the denomination and gone to another, telling the new church that I had abandoned the home. They accepted him as their pastor, yet I knew that his ungodly lifestyle was not God's will for his life. I was upset to know that my children had to see the life of their father with that kind of role model. Nevertheless, I knew in my heart that we all have to give account to God someday for our walk of life.

What did I have to do on a daily basis? I had to...

1. ***Confess and surrender every experience and emotion to the Lord***

2. ***Allow Him to minister inner healing with His unconditional love***

3. ***Forgive others as He forgives me***

4. ***Allow God's love to take the place of all my wounds***

5. ***Pray and bask in the presence of the Lord***

Although many days were filled with forgiveness and other days with unforgiveness, I continued to surrender on a daily basis and that roller coaster of emotions began to balance and stabilize until forgiveness was being experienced more and more as the broken rib was being healed.

Restored from a Broken Rib

I had to take the following steps of restoration and growth in my spiritual, emotional and mental life in order to get into position to begin to walk towards my destiny.

1. *Leave the Past behind you and begin to renew your mind.*

   Phil. 3:13-14 says,

   "Brothers, I do not consider myself yet to have taken hold of it. But one thing I do: Forgetting what is behind and straining toward what is ahead, I press on toward the goal to win the prize for which God has called me heavenward in Christ Jesus."

We must get the knowledge of God's truth in us; renew our minds with His Word, and then use the weapons of *II Cor. 10:4-5* to… *tear down strongholds and every high and lofty thing that exalts itself against the knowledge of God".*

2. *Grow in the Present and seek direction from the Holy Spirit*

   Col. 1:10 declares,

   "And we pray this in order that you may live a life worthy of the Lord and may please him in every way: bearing fruit in every good work, growing in the knowledge of God."

   II Pet. 3:18 says,

   "But grow in the grace and knowledge of our Lord and Savior Jesus Christ. To him be glory both now and forever! Amen."

We must abide or continue in the Word until it becomes revelation given by inspiration of the Holy Spirit. There are newer modern versions of the Bible that will help you to understand the scriptures better, but when the revelation comes, you will know in your heart and mind that the Holy Spirit opened the eyes of your heart to understand the things of the Spirit.

3. *Reach for your Destiny and stand firm.*

    Jer. 29:11 tells us,

    "For I know the plans I have for you, declares the Lord, plans to prosper you and not to harm you, plans to give you hope and a future."

    I Cor. 15:58 states,

    "Therefore, my dear brothers, stand firm. Let nothing move you. Always give yourselves fully to the work of the Lord, because you know that your labor in the Lord is not in vain."

From Restoration to Revelation

The truth is always revealed through the Word of God. We have to learn to accept it and not allow our past to negatively affect the rest of our life. Our past might explain our suffering, but we must not use it as an excuse to stay in bondage. God gives us directions of restoration and we have our victory if we're willing to go all the way, whatever it takes in Jesus' name. *I Cor. 10:13* promises us that…

> *"God will not allow us to be tempted beyond what we can bear, but with every temptation, He will also provide the way out…"*

Joyce Meyer in her book, <u>Battlefield of the Mind,</u> tells us that you cannot have a positive life and a negative mind. Your life will not come in line with God's purpose until your mind does. Remember what ***Proverbs 23:7*** says?

> ***"For as you think in your heart, so are you."***

That means that wrong, negative thoughts will not allow us to walk in the Spirit. Your walk will fulfill His vision and revelation of your purpose. You can walk forward, backwards, or stand still. Again, the choice is yours. Your walk depends on your talking and your talking depends on your hearing. If you hear God's Word and begin to speak it, you will certainly begin to walk it. How much you hear and meditate on God's Word and how much you speak and confess God's Word will determine how much you walk in His divine plan for your life.

Ps. 86:11 declares, ***"Teach me your way, O Lord, and I will walk in your truth…"***

Your mission in life is like crossing the sea. In life, you'll find the smiling sunshine, the clear blue sky, the calm waters, and the favorable breezes. But, you'll also find dark clouds, storms, angry waves and rough adverse winds. Sometimes, the climate can be very unpredictable. When we *"go"* through life, we need to learn to totally depend on God. In Greek, the word *"go"* means *"to go through, to pass through, or to pierce through"*. We can count on His controlling power in the time of danger or trouble. The angry waves will hit our boat. Water will even gush into the boat, but you will not sink while Jesus is in the boat with you. ***Psalms 34:19*** states:

> ***"Many are the afflictions of the just, but God will deliver you of them all."***

Satan cannot destroy your mission, calling, vision, dream or God's purpose for which you were called. Remember that your purpose will affect the purpose of your children and your grandchildren. You are a blessed woman of God! Your children and grandchildren will be blessed. Hallelujah! *Isaiah 43:19* states,

> *"I am doing a new thing! Now it springs up; do you not perceive it? I am making a way in the desert and steams in the wasteland."*

God will make a way during your time of transition, in the midst of your doubt, confusion, anger, loneliness and fear. These feelings will slowly disappear as you place your trust in Him. Just stand and when all else fails, continue to stand. God will honor your faithfulness. He will open a new path when there seems to be none. He is saying to you right now, *"I'm going to deliver you and heal you. I'm going to renew you and release you. I'm going to tell you who you really are, my daughter."* When you come to Jesus as your Lord, He will cause you to stand in His strength. You will know how important you are to Him. Part of your recovery is to learn how to stand up and live in the "*now*" of life instead of the "*then*" of yesterday. That was the "*past*", but this is your "*present*". Allow me to make a declaration of faith into your life.

> *"I proclaim and declare healing to go into your heart and mind right now. I prophecy life and deliverance to you in the name of Jesus! He is rebuilding your self-esteem, your self-respect and your integrity now. Restoration is being activated in your entire being and victory is yours. Receive it in the mighty name of Jesus of Nazareth! You will recover your losses you suffered and get back everything that was stolen from you. Allow His power and anointing to touch the hurting places. He*

knows you've thought about the woman you would have been, the woman you should have been, or the woman you could have been. God is healing and restoring her in you as you call out to Him. The enemy wanted to change your destiny through a series of adverse events in your life, but God will restore you to wholeness and use the circumstances to come against the enemy by ministering to those that are going through the pain that you've gone through. The triumphant woman is coming forth to where she belongs. I'm placing upon you the garment of praise instead of the spirit of heaviness. I'm placing your crown of authority over your head and your robe of righteousness over your shoulders. I give to you the scepter of favor and place it in your hand. You are ready to rule and reign with Christ in the place that He has assigned to you in Jesus' name!"

Isa. 61:3 says the Spirit is upon the Lord and has sent Him:

> *"to bestow a crown of beauty instead of ashes, the oil of gladness instead of mourning and a garment of praise instead of a spirit of despair..."*

No matter what you have suffered, you can hold up your head and walk like a queen.

Psalms 24:9-10 tells you:

> *"Lift up your heads, O ye gates; even lift them up, ye everlasting doors; and the King of glory."*

Position Yourself for Greatness

I received great enlightenment when I read Mike Murdock's comment on the chapter on *"Enemies"* from the <u>Wisdom</u>

<u>Commentary 1</u>. He states *"When God has used up the benefits of your present season, He assigns an enemy to become your exit from that season."*[2] I had never looked at my situation in that way because according to God's Word, marriage is for life. But the word missing in my phrase is *"Godly"* and therefore should read, *"Godly marriage is for life"*. It needs to be a Godly marriage, a healthy marriage, not one that I had experienced. Whether you agree with me or not, I actually believe that God moved me into my next season through an adversary, in this case, my husband. I was actually delivered from destruction through divorce. Pain in my past circumstances with no change in the present was necessary to give birth to the dream God was developing in my life. It allowed humility to come into my life and humility attracts God and his angels to work on your behalf.

You have unlimited access to all of God's promises which are legally yours by birthright in Christ Jesus.

Galatians 3:29 tells us:

> ***"If you belong to Christ, then you're Abraham's seed, and heirs according to the promise."***

II Pet. 1:3 tells us clearly:

> ***"According to his divine power hath given us all things that pertain unto life and godliness..."***

You have inherited power, prosperity and protection. ***Deut. 28:1-13*** lists thirty-one promises alone.

Here are a few scriptures on the three types of promises.

- **Promises of Power**

  Matt. 10:1 – *"... he gave them authority..."*
  Acts 1:8 – *"but you will receive power..."*

- **Promises of Prosperity**

  II Chron. 1:12 – "…*I will give you wealth, riches and honor…*"

  Matt. 6:33 – "…*all these things will be given to you…*"

- **Promises of Protection**

  Ex. 15:26 – "…*I am the Lord who heals you…*"

  II Tim. 4:18 – "*The Lord will rescue me from every evil attack…*"

When you allow the promises to operate in your life, then the fruit of the Spirit will automatically begin to operate. How do the promises operate in your life? Begin by following these steps to get into position for your destiny.

1. *Know your position in Christ and Christ's position in you.*

   Gal. 2:20 says:

   "*I have been crucified with Christ and I no longer live, but Christ lives in me. The life I live in the body, I live by faith in the Son of God, who loved me and gave himself for me.*"

   Gal. 4:7 tells us:

   "*So you are no longer a slave, but a son; and since you are a son, God has also made you an heir.*"

   For this, you have to be willing to crucify your fleshly carnal desires. The "*me*" has to die and allow Christ to live. After you have analyzed your circumstances and tried to understand its origin, it will take the authority of God's Word to put the past under your feet. But, don't give up!

No matter how bad the condition of your life is, you can regain the territory the devil has stolen from you. I know you're paying the consequences for someone else's decisions, but you will regain your position, little by little, with your faith and trust in God, your Restorer. Then, all of a sudden, when you least expect it, the day will come, just like in the life of Joseph, that God will do the miracle of placing you in the position for which you were called. We will learn to lean on God's grace and not on our own ability to get the desired results.

God promises in *Isa. 43:2-3*:

"When you pass through the waters, I will be with you, and through the river, they will not overwhelm you. When you walk through the fire, you will not be burned or scorched, nor will the flame kindle upon you. For I, the Lord, am your God. I, the Holy One of Israel your Savior…"

2. *Make yourself available to God.*

   Isa. 6:8 declares:

   "Then I heard the voice of the Lord saying, "Whom shall I send and who will go for us?" And I said, "Here I am. Send me!"

The enemy will try to remind you of your past and the long-range aftereffects of past pain, but when you make yourself available to God and all He has for you and your future, don't waste your time meditating on your past. Think about your future. The problem might be rooted in the past, but your victory is in the present. Take what

God's Word says for you "*now*". This encouraging word you are hearing today is able to heal your "*yesterday*". You must participate with God's plan for your life in order to step into the next season He has ordained for you. God will take you from the painful reality of your own grief to the glory of God's restorative plan. So, therefore, position yourself for what God has for you in your future.

3. ***Claim your inheritance and know what you have in Christ.***

The Holy Spirit that dwells in you is designed to help you mature, causing you to grow in the Lord. He indwells us to give us victory over sin, making us holy and lives within us to give us the character of Christ. The Holy Spirit, empowering us, is designed to equip us, enabling us to serve the Lord and gives us tools for ministry, making us effective. Both the indwelling and the empowering of the Holy Spirit are essential if we are to reach our full potential in Christ and reach our destiny. We enter into spiritual warfare by the power of His Spirit, coming against past failures, inadequacies and betrayals that threaten to hold us out of our rightful place and not allow us to be positioned to see the promises of God fulfilled. So, let's fulfill God's purposes and accomplish the destiny for which He created us, by receiving all that the Holy Spirit has provided for us. Joseph's calling involved much more than providing resources in times of deficiency. His true ministry was a threefold anointing typified in ***Gen. 41:40-42*** which states:

"Thou shalt be over my house, and according unto thy word shall all my people be ruled: only in the throne will I be greater than thou. And Pharaoh said

unto Joseph, See, I have set thee over all the land of Egypt. And Pharaoh took off his ring from his hand and arrayed him in vestures of fine linen, and put a gold chain around his neck."

In one day, God placed Joseph in a position of greatness, taking him from the prison to the palace. First, he received the king's ring, illustrating spiritual authority. The ring of authority proclaimed that Joseph had the king's full endorsement. You are a daughter of the King and have the heavenly endorsement from the Father above. Secondly, Joseph was dressed with royal robes, prophetically depicting the priesthood of the Lord, clothed in purity and Christ's nature. Finally, Joseph received a gold chain, exemplifying the prosperity needed to fulfill God's divine plan for his life. You also carry this threefold anointing in the place of greatness that God has designed for you!

1 Pierce, Chuck & Systema, Rebecca Wagner, <u>Possessing your Inheritance</u> (Ventura, CA Renew Books, 1999, p. 69

2 Murdock, Mike, <u>Wisdom Commentary 1</u> (Ft. Worth, TX Wisdom International Publisher, 2002, p. 75

Chapter 4:
Embrace your Giant

*Adverse Circumstances take you Higher

Adverse circumstances come in the size of a giant, at least that's how it seemed to me, because this particular giant was a total new experience in my life. When you've never had to deal with a *"Giant"* like this one before, the *"Giant"* of separation and divorce, life becomes difficult to handle and the idea of your destiny begins to diminish, especially when you thought your marital relationship was supposed to last a lifetime. This *"Giant"* in my life was supposed to be the will of God for me. *How was I to address this conflict when it was to be a lifetime partnership that God had ordained?*

Regardless of the choices of others and how they affect you and your children, you have the option of choosing life or death, blessings or curses, enjoyment or hardships. It doesn't matter what your overwhelming circumstances are, there is a mandate and the power of God for breakthrough. Those that don't know Christ as Savior and Lord have no idea what is available to them for the healing of the soul, thoughts and emotions. This is why it's important for us to share our personal salvation experience with them, in order for them to have this wonderful relationship with the God who is available to heal every wound.

Look at your Giant straight in the Eyes

As hard as this might seem, don't be afraid of your giant. Confront your giant! You have inner strength within you that only begins to develop with adverse circumstances, whatever they might be. You are not alone through the journey. Your mind must stay healthy, thinking that you're going to get through this storm with your trust totally in God, because His grace is sufficient in your weakness.

Your children need to know that you love them very much, regardless of the circumstances. They must know that the divorce is not their fault. The enemy will try to drop this thought into their mind. Make sure you speak to them about this matter. This is the time to demonstrate your love, care and concern for them as never before. This family situation will negatively impact their academics and interfere with their concentration in school. So, keep in contact with their teachers and check their schoolwork daily, because they need to continue moving forward, succeeding with their educational goals. They will think about life's circumstances while at school, so you need to be praying for them. If you notice a change in their grades or the teacher shares concerns, make sure you are there to give your children all of the support they need. The school should provide help with tutoring if needed. Make it a point to work on their self-esteem as an ongoing goal. It's important for them to have good friends and for them to be involved in activities that will keep them focused on their physical, mental and spiritual development and growth. Even though you might think you don't have the strength to endure and you feel emotionally and mentally drained, take care of yourself. No one is going to take care of you, but you. Although you might have a wonderful support group (family and friends) that will be there for you, they can't be there every moment of the day. When discouragement sets in and you ask yourself questions like *"How can this be happening to me?"* or *"I don't deserve this. I've been faithful and the best wife I could be"*, know in your heart that all this will pass. With time, things will get better, because your destiny awaits you. Think of it this way. Every day that goes by, you're getting closer to your position for destiny.

Embrace your Giant, No Matter What

You need to learn to embrace your giant because it will allow you to go through the process faster and healing will begin to mend your broken heart. In the process, you will hope that reconciliation takes place, but in the worst case scenario where that is not an option any longer, you have to let go of that relationship in order to step through your door of destiny. **Your life is not over**! If you could only see through the eyes of God, you would move with greater motivation towards your destiny.

I had experienced religious abuse associated with distortions of headship and submission, not only in my marriage, but also in my church denomination. I had to pray and forgive each one of the executive leaders of the district executive board for not using the wisdom or the spiritual gifts of God to reconcile our marriage. I thought they had spiritual character. You see, under the Jewish dispensation, the high priest had inscribed in jeweled letters on a golden frontlet: "*Holiness to the Lord*." So every preacher in Christ's ministry must be molded into and mastered by this same holy motto. It is a shame for a minister of the Kingdom to fall lower in holiness of character and holiness of aim than the Jewish priesthood. For the man that does not make prayer an important factor is his own life and ministry is weak in God's work and powerless in fulfilling God's cause in the world as His vessel. But now, I understand, it was God delivering me from devastation through divorce. No one could be the best husband for me, except the Bridegroom himself, my Lord and Savior!

My dream changed because new opportunities and connections awaited me, which were planned by God. You don't know if it was for this reason that your purpose began to take a new shape, which is perhaps to help others that are going through similar circumstances. Whatever the reason, in time everything will begin to take shape and the pieces of the puzzle will begin to be placed together, one piece at a time.

The Giant will Fall, Never to Rise Again

A new future with an entire new freedom to be "*you*" begins to form. It is of the utmost importance that your attitude stays positive. My repetitive prayer during the time of transition was and continues to be, *"My life is in your hands, Lord."* I knew that God had a plan and "*divorce*" wasn't making me less of a person, regardless of what society or the church believes. Unless you go through a similar experience, you really don't know what that experience is. Others won't understand your feelings, unless they've gone through a similar trauma in their own life. But there is "*One*" who has gone through rejection and betrayal from all mankind. He was victorious and has given us the position and power to be victorious as well, if we believe in Him.

Philippians 4:13 says:

> *"I can do all things through Christ, who strengthens me."*

You can begin to take steps toward your future with Christ as your new Husband. He will never leave you or forsake you. He will never abandon you or leave you alone to take on life's challenges with no one to turn to. He is ever present in your life. He has assigned His angels to minister to you and your children. He is preparing you, His chosen vessel of honor to be used for His glory.

David cut off the head of Goliath in the name of the Lord and the Philistines began to flee because they were afraid. You can cut off the head of worthlessness and rejection in your life by taking the following steps of healing. Your enemies will flee and be scattered because they will see the mighty Spirit of God working on your behalf.

Steps to Inner Healing and Victory

1. **Shake it off daily, never to return and when it does, shake if off again.**

The term "*shake it off*" refers to letting go of something. Let go of those things in your life that are holding you back from moving in the direction that God desires you to go. Yes, it will be a process, but shake if off daily. Although this process of "*shaking it off*" has more to do with your attitude, sometimes you have to go deeper in order to get to those areas deep within that need healing. You need to learn to cry out to Him with an ineffable cry of self-despair and self-helplessness until God's power and fire comes in and fills, purifies, and empowers your soul to be free again. The temple should be held sacred for God. For this, there is a great price to be paid; death to self in order for God to rule in the holy of holies of your temple. Begin to dream again and make sure that God is your dream partner. Begin to trust God at a higher level of trust. This will be a process that needs time, but it's not impossible to achieve that higher level of trust in the Lord.

Too many women completely place their trust in their husband because they've given their life to their partner, expecting him to love and protect her "*until death do us part*". The secret to leading a happy life is to know that God is the only one that can bring true happiness to your life. Happiness is a decision within, regardless of whether others, including your husband, value you or not. When you learn to give value to your own life because of God's purpose for bringing you into this world, then you'll have a true reason to live and have the passion to fulfill that purpose. I will be bold enough to say that many wives place their husband on a pedestal, which is idolatry. Although he is the one who works to support the family, which is his God-given role, he is not a god. In this time and age, many wives are also working outside of the home to help with the finances. We applaud all of the single moms and dads that have to carry out both roles in the home. May God richly bless you and strengthen you in all of your endeavors.

We need to be thankful for all of the wonderful men that are fulfilling their role day after day, providing for their family. It's challenging to follow through with this responsibility without the Lord or his helpmeet. As women, we were created to help our husband and God equipped us for that purpose. Yet, there are many women that don't know how to fulfill that position and many men that don't know how to handle the giftedness of their wife. This is where jealousy and strife take place, especially when there's very little good ongoing communication and support one for the other. Miscommunication happens a lot with couples in the church because the man uses the term *"submission"* (**Eph. 5:22**) as a weapon, yet the Word of God speaks of *"submitting one to another"*.

> **"Submit to one another out of reverence for Christ."**
> **Eph. 5:21**

As surprising as it might be to you, statistics tell us that even in the church, the percentage of divorce is equal to the percentage of divorce outside of the church. The enemy is dividing the family by dividing the marriage. When the marriage vows are broken, it creates a negative impact on the church and its ability to be the example of the victorious life. But, we are in the last days and the enemy is using all of the strategies needed to keep the Bride, which is the Church, from being prepared for that day when the Bridegroom will return for His Bride. The Church has been going through the process of restoration for centuries after the Early Church lost her power of impact due to persecution and historical figures that changed the course of history for the Church. But, the Church ministry will be restored before His coming and although the enemy will use every vehicle possible to destroy the Church, the Bride of Christ will prevail!

If the destroyer of our soul can reach the family of the Pastor, then imagine how this impacts the Church and stops it from moving forward to reach her destiny, which is to share the Gospel with the community and to give for the salvation of souls around the world as they give to ministries on the foreign field. Cast yourself unreservedly upon God; yield yourself wholly to Him. He will accomplish all that your faith has laid upon Him. When you realize that God has given you a divine task, He'll assume the responsibility of removing the obstacles which stand between you and the task. That giant can be an attack of sickness, limited financial resources, a broken relationship or a number of countless experiences that hit us in life. These difficulties are a test of our faith in God and challenge us to stay faithful to our Savior, regardless of the circumstances that come our way. They lead us to a deeper and truer appreciation of our dependence upon God. It's time to remove our focus on how these adverse circumstances are affecting us and our children and place our sight on God's strength to get us through the storm, for beyond the dark clouds lies the rainbow. During this time of refocus in your life, you will begin to experience inner healing. It's going to take just as much effort, if not more, to maintain your restoration in order to perceive God's direction for your life. God is putting all of the pieces of the puzzle together, bringing people as those divine connections that will lead you to your destiny. Perhaps you're thinking, "*This is going to be too difficult.*" Yes, it's not going to be easy, but it can be done in Jesus' name. How long will it take? It'll take as long as it takes for you to get totally restored and on your way towards your destiny. So, get ready for your miraculous journey. Your fruit of patience will need to be manifested in your emotions and thoughts as the days go by and each day will be a day closer to fulfilling your destiny.

The best way to receive each challenging day is by offering your praise to the *"One"* who deserves all honor and glory for taking you through your transition. As you desire to hear the voice of God as your new Husband, it's important that God hears your voice as well. You are sowing seeds of adoration in the heavens with your words of praise and worship. You're going through the labor pains now and the contractions are extremely painful, but you will give birth to your miracle and your dream will come forth in due season. Praise and worship are strong weapons that will help you to overcome your natural feelings of confusion and despair and move you into the supernatural realm of His presence. It's a living sacrifice of praise you offer when your flesh tells you there's nothing to praise Him for, especially when you're in the middle of heartache and you can hardly carry your pain. Yet, you praise Him anyway. Believe me; God is delivering you from a lifetime of heartache, belittling, violence, betrayal, deception and unfaithfulness. Thank God for being your Deliverer, your Provider, your Comforter and your Peace! There's nothing like being in His Presence and allowing Him to remove those burdens in your heart and soul.

2. Walk a life of consistent obedience and don't forget to use your spiritual weapons

David picked up small stones to be used for his slingshot, which was his weapon against Goliath, the enemy of Israel.

You have spiritual stones of weaponry that will enable you to confront your enemy. Here are your Victory stones:

- *Your weapons: the Word, praise & worship, prayer*
- *Your position: Holy Spirit authority*
- *Your attack: The name of the Lord*
- *Your victory: Head of the Giant*

Satan's plan is to destroy your righteousness because you are a daughter of the King. You have not only been called to be His child, but His Servant, His Chosen Vessel and His Bride. Righteousness means to be in the right standing before God. According to **Isaiah 54:14**, the enemy will try to come against you in three different ways.

> *"In righteousness you will be established, you will be far from oppression; for you will not fear: and far from terror; for it will not come near you."*

First, he will try to come against you with oppression. Oppression in Hebrew means *"distress"*, which is an attack on the body. *Second,* he will try to come against you with fear. The word "fear" in this context means *"to be afraid"* and fear produces doubt and unbelief, which is an attack on the soul, which includes your thoughts and emotions. Third, the enemy will try to come against you with terror. Terror in Hebrew means *"destruction"*, which is an attack on the spirit. The enemy will try to attack you in one dimension, because it'll lead to other realms of your being and you could actually be attacked on all three levels if you allow it. When the enemy tempted Jesus when He was in the desert, Satan attacked him in His body, soul and spirit. First, the enemy tempted Jesus by commanding Him to change the stones to be made bread. This was an attack on His body. Jesus had been fasting for forty days and forty nights. Then, Satan attacked his soul by telling Him to fall from the pinnacle of the Temple and call the angels to rescue Him, tempting His thoughts, emotions and will. Finally, the devil, after showing Jesus all of the kingdoms of the world from the highest part of the mountain, tempted Jesus to worship him. This was an attack on His spirit, that area that was created to worship our Creator. In all three accounts, Jesus responded by saying, *"It is written."* We can use the same Word of God to respond to the enemy of our soul in our circumstances.

My dad died in the year 2000 and since then I've had a couple of nightmares where my dad is demonstrating his uncontrollable temper, experiences I suffered in my childhood. These nightmares reveal that my life was affected and left lasting scars. Although I have applied the blood of Jesus over my memory, these kinds of experiences could have been avoided. I understand that our parents did the best they could with what they knew, but our natural tendency is to repeat with our children what we have learned and experienced as children. Some parents behave with dysfunction because they're passing on unhealthy experiences that they learned from their parents. But, when it is inappropriate behavior, there's got to be some kind of intervention to break the cycle of dysfunction. It has to stop in order for you and your children to enjoy God's blessings of abundance in every area of your lives. Don't allow the enemy's attack of oppression, fear and terror defeat you. Fight the good fight of faith for your life and the life of your children.

Part of your advocating for your children is for the atmosphere in your home during your transition. There should be an atmosphere in your home of feeling *"connected"*, no matter what conflicts exist. Safety in the family means that your children feel assured that they are loved by you, no matter what. They also need to feel safe in your home and not have feelings of chaos or confusion. Above all, they need to feel loved by you.

Sometimes we're unaware that we're demonstrating signs of anger and discontent because of the situation we're going through and indirectly, we're punishing our kids with our own behavior. My children were 4, 8, and 14 years old when I took the step to make a change from our life of hardship. I remember that although it was not my intention to treat them unjustly, now I realize I had deficits in my emotions and would sometimes show emotional withdrawal, where I would detach myself from the children because I didn't want them to notice the pain and anger I was experiencing. I had to learn to cry before the Lord when they were not there and ask God for inner strength to get me through the day. These kinds of reactions can seriously undermine a child's ability to feel secure in who he is. The family needs to feel bonded and feel the loving, caring attachment because the children will not feel that they are part of a complete family since one of the members is missing. I had to teach my children that our family was complete and whole because Jesus stepped in as my Husband and He was now the center of our home and family. Jesus had been there all the time, but now He was taking on a new role in our lives like never before. I had to pray for their dad; that God would bestow mercy on him and show him what God's plan was for his life.

Divorce is like a living death because there is a death in the relationship between a couple, yet both continues to live without each other. Some couples cooperate because of the children and due to forgiveness; they get on with their lives. Some couples actually become friends after their divorce.

But when the spouse doesn't cooperate, it feels like the loss of a loved one, yet the person is still alive. To get a better understanding of marriage types, you need to understand the four general husband types:

4 Kinds of Husbands

1.	**Cooperative and saved** • This man is a mature man of God. • He recognizes the importance of God's will.	Prov. 21:21 *"He who pursues righteousness and love finds life, prosperity and honor.*
2.	**Cooperative and Unsaved** • This man recognizes the importance of a relationship with God. • He lacks commitment with God .	I Pet. 3:1-2 *"Wives, in the same way, be submissive to your husbands so that, if any of them do not believe the Word, they may be won over without words by the behavior of their wives, when they see the purity and reverence of your lives."*
3.	**Saved and Uncooperative** • This man is an immature Christian. • He is jealous & insecure.	I Pet. 2:19 *"For it is commendable if a man (woman) bears up under the pain of unjust suffering because he/she is conscious of God."*
4.	**Unsaved and uncooperative** • This man is deceived by Satan. • He is possessive; manipulator.	I Pet. 3:14-15 *"But even if you should suffer for what is right, you are blessed. Do not fear what they fear; do not be frightened. But in your hearts set apart Christ as Lord."*

The enemy takes advantage of the circumstances and the attack is on, but we still stand, knowing that we have an Advocate.

I John 2:1 tells us:

> *"...we have one that speaks to the Father in our defense-Jesus Christ, the Righteous One."*

The enemy will not be silent. He will try to attack you in all three areas of your created being. Oppression, fear and terror will talk to your thoughts that the enemy will throw your way.

Isaiah 54:15 states:

> *"Behold, they shall surely gather together, but not by me; whosoever will gather together against you will fall for your sake."*

But the promise is found in verse 17 where God declares:

> *"No weapon that is formed against you will prosper, and every tongue that will rise against you in judgment you will condemn. This is the heritage of the servants of the Lord and their righteousness is from me, says the Lord."*

We have authority to *"condemn their tongue"*. You can speak to your giant (mountain) as stated in *Mark 11:23-24*:

> *"For verily I say unto you, whosoever shall say to this mountain (giant), Be thou removed, and be thou cast into the sea; and shall not doubt in his heart, but shall believe that those things which he says shall come to pass, he will have whatever he says. Therefore, I say*

unto you, whatever things you desire, when you pray, believe that you have received them and you shall have them."

Come against the enemy with these three different scriptures:

1. *Acts 10:38* - **Speak to the oppression**

    "God anointed Jesus of Nazareth with the Holy Spirit and with power; who went about doing good and healing all that were oppressed of the devil; for God was with him."

During the night when you're all alone, especially on those nights when the children are not with you, speak to your giant of loneliness and tell him that God is ever present. You are not alone because the One that created you has assigned His angels to minister to you even in the darkest hours of the night.

2. *II Tim. 1:7* - **Speak to the fear**

    "God has not given us the spirit of fear, but of power, and of love, and of a sound mind."

When you have to go to court for another session, walk in like a queen, because as a daughter of the Most High God, you are preparing for your wedding day with your Bridegroom. Although in the physical realm, you're walking into a courtroom, in the spiritual realm, you are walking in heavenly places. You are royalty and one day you'll be living in your mansion that God has prepared for you. So speak to the fear with boldness and say, *"I will not be afraid for God's love is greater than any fear that the enemy will throw my way.*

I will trust in God, my Deliverer". Although Joseph was in prison, God saw him as second in command to Pharaoh. You've got to see yourself as a woman of excellence because that is your position in God.

3. *Ps. 91:5-7* - **Speak to the terror**

> ***"You will not be afraid for the terror by night or for the arrow that flies by day, nor for the pestilence that walks in darkness, nor for the destruction that wastes at noonday. A thousand shall fall at your side, and ten thousand at your right hand, but it will not come near you."***

Speak to the terror with all of your heart and don't be afraid. Say, *"How dare you, devil, try to destroy my life when God has the very best for me. You can't have my life or the lives of my children. Our lives belong to God. You go now in the name of Jesus."* Remember that greater is He that is within you, which is the Holy Spirit of God.

Because you've embraced your giant by going to battle in the name of the Lord, God will give you victory. Keep your focus off the circumstances and focus on God and His infallible Word. God wants you to enter a new dimension of His delivering power. Although time is a healing factor in life, time by itself does not heal the wounds from the past. Time has to be accompanied by active, purposeful steps toward healing, including forgiveness and a halt to repeating the past. If the past continues to be rehearsed, we cannot move forward towards our destiny because there has to be an end in order for there to be a new beginning. It's challenging for a wounded individual to give out life, peace, love joy, forgiveness, reconciliation and wholeness when he/she has none to give. This is why it is so important to take care of our mind and our heart. Our actions are a direct result of our thoughts. If we have a negative mind, we will have a negative life. If, on the other hand, we renew our mind according to God's Word, we will experience" *the good and acceptable and perfect will of God"* for our lives (*Rom. 12:2*). So, let's use our spiritual battle weapons in order to minister life to others.

My Battle Weapons of Warfare

As you begin to battle in your spirit, know that you have resources to help you. You cannot take this journey alone. You have the spoken Word of God, the application of the Blood of Jesus, your prayer language, your walk of obedience and the Name of Jesus. I had to use all of these spiritual resources as I went through my battle and continue to conduct myself as a spiritual warrior. I must confess that I did not use them to the best of my ability due to the wounds in my heart, but I did what I could with the revelation knowledge I had in that season in my life. This is why I want to share that you must take advantage of all that God has to offer you through His Spirit. It's part of your inheritance and will make a difference in your life.

When everything started coming out in the open in the church, the leaders and church members were so confused with what they saw as a serious marriage problem between the pastor and his wife. They couldn't believe what was happening. I imagine the church people were asking the leadership for explanations in regards to what was occurring Sunday after Sunday. Many were asking themselves, *"How could the man of God not talk to his wife?"* Others commented, *"You can't touch the anointed one." "What in the world is going on?"* others asked. These were some of the questions and comments the disappointed people of the church expressed in trying to find a solution. For those of you that have gone through a similar experience, I want to share with you that you are not without spiritual resources in the battle. You must remember:

*__You are not alone__.

Think of the heroes in the Word of God that had similar struggles. Remember that we have the Holy Spirit who is ready with the power that abides within our temple. We only have to take our steps of action in faith. God says in **I Cor. 10:13**: *"The wrong desires that come into your life aren't anything new and different. Many others have faced exactly the same problems before you."*

*__There is hope__.

A fresh start and a new hope are always available. God already knew you were going to go through your experience with all of your pain. But, He also had the solution and way of escape planned for you. He will not allow you to go through any experience that is too difficult for you to bear without His divine help.

*__God will help you through your time of transition__.

The Holy Spirit is ready to begin to take you through your new journey with Him. Seek a new depth in your relationship with God. Continue to commit to living a holy life, free from the past. Stay focused on your future. During this time, God is conducting spiritual surgery, allowing the anointing of the Spirit of revelation to quicken and make alive the Word of Truth necessary to replace seeds of corruption with the dominion of His divine attributes.

Allow Him to take hold of your hand, for He will walk with you all along the way.

Even to this day, the father of my children chooses not to speak to me and blames me for everything, but I cannot control his will to "let go" and "let God". Although there is unfinished business, I cannot change anything when the other party is not willing to cooperate. So again, I surrender everything over to God. He is in charge of my life. I've taken the necessary steps to confront, release and resolve issues in my life to the best of my ability and with the help of the Holy Spirit; I have hope for my future. As I look to my future, I must be alert to the presence of the enemy and be aware of his strategies to discourage me from what God has for me in my future and the future of my sons. I must remain fervent in prayer, never hesitating to call upon God for my every need. I will follow the path of obedience no matter how intense the pressure. I will praise and worship Him in the good times and the bad times, in the present and in future years to come as long as I am alive. I will trust His Word regardless of my circumstances. He has taken me through the most difficult situations in my life and with the same grace, mercy, and tender loving care, He will do the same for you. You see, it's not about me or you. It's all about Him and His perfect will. He's using these life's experiences to help you grow and mature in your relationship with Him in order to fulfill your destiny. He wants to use you in such a great way, but you must be ready to be used in the way that He desires to use you. Because of our emotional ties, it's difficult for women to let go of the past. But, this is not the hour to look back at past failures and old wounds. When you keep looking back, you're losing your focus on coming into your next victory. Let God deal with the past because He will judge it. You need to move into the best that is yet ahead for your life. Jesus is telling women what he told the woman in *John 8:10-11* when He said, ***"Woman, has no one condemned you? Neither do I condemn you."*** He is saying to let the condemnation of the past be removed from you. "*Let it go my daughter, so I can begin to use you in a new way. I'm going to use women in such a way that it will change the course of the earth. I will clothe you with a favor so that you can advance in a new way. It is a new day,*" says the Lord.

Mike Murdock shares in his book, <u>Wisdom Commentary1</u> about a visit to Lagos, Nigeria and how his friend, who is a Bishop shared the following which will help you:

- ***Gratitude provokes Joy***
- ***Joy provokes Praise***
- ***Praise provokes His Divine Presence***

Sometimes, it takes life's difficult experiences to get to the point of understanding His way to mold our lives in order to reach our assignment here on earth. God is not done with you or me yet. As long as we're alive here on planet earth, there is a plan for us to accomplish and He will help us to fulfill His plan and purpose in our lifetime. ***Jude, verses 24-25*** says:

> ***"To Him who is able to keep you from falling and to present you before His glorious presence without fault and with great joy – to the only God our Savior be glory, majesty, power and authority, through Jesus Christ our Lord, before all ages, now and forevermore!***

Chapter 5:
It's Time to Recuperate your Inheritance

*Becoming the true "*Me*" I was Meant to Be

All of us that have called on the name of Jesus and accepted Him as personal Savior are adopted into the family of God and are heirs according to the promise and as heirs are given the birthright of our inheritance in Christ Jesus. We are all given our "*portion*" as promised by God according to the covenant. When the enemy dares to touch one of God's children for the sole purpose of being God's child, he will try every strategy to draw us away from our heavenly Father because of our inheritance in Christ. Besides being a child of the living God, we have a purpose in this world of bringing the lost into the kingdom of God. When that holy call is upon your life and especially when you are being obedient to His call, the conflict increases and attacks are on the rise. But, regardless of the enemy's attack, we are still heirs and have the right to our inheritance.

You are destined to recover your blessings according to *Deut. 7:11-13:*

> *"Therefore, take care to follow the commands, decrees and laws I give you today. If you pay attention to these laws and are careful to follow them, then the Lord your God will keep his covenant of love with you, as he swore to your forefathers. He will love you and bless you and multiply you..."*

On the other side of divorce (your mountain), exists your inheritance of peace, joy, love and blessings you cannot imagine. The Word of God tells us that you have a double portion coming to you.

Zechariah 9:12 declares:

> *"...Even now I announce that I will restore twice as much to you."*

When the enemy endeavors to pursue his plans of destruction, as a daughter of the Most High God, you have the right to a double portion. Our portion is sometimes tested and seems to be lost, but we must not assume that God has either forgotten or forsaken us. We must stay focused on who God is and know that He is working on our behalf. We must also be assured that somewhere in our loss, God has a plan of blessing, restoration, and multiplication. Although it seems that your blessings tarry, they will come because God has promised it in His Word. God told Abraham, *"I will bless you... and your inheritance will be like the stars in the sky"*, which Abraham could not possibly count. His inherited blessings passed on to future generations because of the promise of the seed. Even if you don't see your promise in your lifetime, as long as you continue to speak His Word and believe, God is able to bless you through the seed of your children. *How will those blessings come?* Blessings of multiplication come when you're committed to your relationship to God and committed to His plan and purpose. If you receive revelation about sowing seed or giving, you can release your faith to receive your promises through the words of your mouth. I wish I had this deeper revelation earlier in life in order to believe in a greater way for my circumstances. Receive the instruction of the Lord and apply the Truth to your situation in this season of your life. You have the best Helper, the Holy Spirit, to take you from one spiritual dimension to another, from one level of spiritual growth to another, from glory to glory. Whenever there's a plan, there is a design and strategy to fulfill that plan. Sometimes there are detours, U-turns, and railroad crossings where you have to wait for a while. But in His timing, God will enable, enlighten, and empower you to fulfill His plan.

My grandmother, Lolita Flores Medina, was called into ministry at a young age while living in San Antonio, Texas. Although both grandparents served as leaders in the church, the enemy had a plan to steal their divine call from God. My grandfather began to stray from God's path, leaving the family to take on unnecessary burdens. My grandmother struggled with her marriage and decided to move to Chicago, Illinois when my parents answered the call to ministry. My parents planted new Hispanic churches in the Midwest area of the United States. My grandmother became a leader with the denomination and led the Women's Missionary Council. She visited the churches, organizing the women's ministry groups. My mother, Delia Medina Mora, was also called into ministry. After moving to California years later, she led Women's Ministries on the Pacific Coast, ministering in conventions, retreats, Missionette camps and church rallies. My mother had the privilege of ministering to thousands of women throughout her many years of service, not only in the United States, but Mexico, Central and South America as well through the many trips she took, speaking at conventions and conferences. She was also on the radio, ministering throughout Latin America with her program segment entitled "*An Appointment with God*".

The enemy knew that she was a chosen vessel, useful for the work of the Lord, impacting thousands of lives for the Kingdom of God. Due to such a strong call on her life, the enemy planned strategies of interruption and adversity within the marriage. Although my father planted churches and many souls were saved through his ministry, he had a weakness that the enemy was ready to expose. Regardless of the circumstances, she learned to totally depend on the Lord to intervene, hoping he would change. She moved forward towards her destiny even with a lack of commitment on his part. We can't ignore our history, but we can realign our future with God's help.

The women in my family have experienced enormous difficulties in their lives, but I'm proud to say that these women have stood faithful in their walk with God and have demonstrated the role of a chosen vessel of faith and honor. They disciplined themselves to be strong, regardless of the challenges in their life and gave all honor and glory to the King, their Deliverer. These women have been brave in their endeavors to reach their destiny and I salute them for being faithful to their divine call of God. If God allowed them to reach their destiny and touch the lives of many, He can do the same for you and me.

God created us as women first before he made us a wife, mother or minister. We are His special creation and according to the scriptures, we are the temple of the Holy Spirit, the apple of His eye, His special treasure, His chosen generation and His royal priesthood. No one has the right to violate the temple of the Holy Spirit, physically, mentally or emotionally. Even the law provides protection against domestic violence and forms of abuse against women and children. But people seem to think because the pastor is a man of God; we can't allow the authorities to get involved when there's a serious problem. Let us remember that even if that person is the pastor or a leader of the church, first of all he is a man. These dysfunctional men will continue to demonstrate the same ungodly behavior until they are "*stopped*" from bringing ongoing harm to their families. Although it may be difficult to make this decision, especially when dealing with our husband and father of our children, something needs to be done to break the cycle! Otherwise, the cycle of dysfunction will continue generation after generation. You can't stay in that kind of relationship that will affect your life and the lives of your children for the rest of their lives. A man or woman that demonstrates dysfunction needs professional help and deliverance with the help of God. God will use you to deliver your children from these unnecessary experiences and memories. God will provide an abundance of grace and love to get them through their journey as well. You children's future is in the hands of God, but He will use you as a mother with His loving nature to develop God's character in the lives of your children, so they can become all that God has called them to be.

I'm so grateful to God for sending His angels to take care of my children and covering them with the protection of God through their transition. He provided a way of escape through the love of a supportive family instead of my children searching for other ways to calm their anxieties about their present and future. I'm so very proud of my three sons for allowing God to intervene in their lives and submitting to His ways.

My oldest son Arty studied and focused on becoming a pilot with American Airlines. He loves God and is pursuing his career with excellence. Because of his profession, God is providing the opportunity for me to travel in order to develop my ministry of the Gospel for which I was called.

My second son Andy will be finishing ITT, Institute of Technology in 2011 and is pursuing his career in Computer Information Systems. He is a very bright young man with a wonderful future ahead of him. He's sensitive to the things of God and I know he'll fulfill his destiny in God.

My third son Aaron will be attending college soon and will be majoring in Engineering. I can see how he has a passion for God and a heart to please the Lord. My prayers have always been that my sons would be apostles and prophets in the marketplace or workforce. They can use their God-given calling wherever God takes them in their career path to fulfill God's plan for their lives. Glory to God! I cannot be more grateful to God for allowing me to see His grace and power move in the lives of my sons. God is good! He can do the same for you!

I realize there are families that go through separation and divorce and sometimes the children don't do very well, especially the teenagers. If that is your case, make sure you get counseling for you and your children. You can contribute to and stimulate recovery more rapidly. There are agencies that offer free services to help you in your situation. Look for reading resources, books that deal with getting through your transition and finding solutions. Find a good church that will support you and show compassion towards your situation. This will help you through the process as you will need as much support as possible. Begin to recover those losses of joy and peace. Love your children more than you've ever loved them. They need your love because your love will help them through their transition. Although you are experiencing anger, don't take it out on them! It's not their fault for how you feel. Don't allow them to blame you for the situation either. Give them a Godly response with wisdom and understanding. Your love will bring them through the transition and you'll be able to take your path to your destiny with love and peace. Look for a good Bible-based church where you find love and support for your family. Remember to share with your children that your family is complete with Jesus as center of your household.

In my case, the problem was between my husband and me and the issue with his controlling character. He grew up in adverse circumstances in Sonora, Mexico when his dad abandoned his mother. He left school to work in order to help raise his brothers and sisters, therefore becoming the *"savior"* of the home. This attitude in the family continued in his life throughout the years and unfortunately entered my life when I married him. Any time he would disagree with my words, decisions or actions, although they were reasonable in my opinion, his character of control negatively impacted our relationship in such a way that emotional and mental abuse was commonplace. But, what do you do when you're a pastor's wife and this dilemma continues year after year? His ungodly response towards me was his *"silent treatment"*, which was a devastating experience. This pattern of behavior continued year after year due to his character that he refused to surrender to God. I believe God was giving him opportunities those sixteen years to mature in that particular area of his life, but he never took one opportunity and our family suffered because of it.

I remember expressing my frustration with my children because I could not express myself freely with their father. Out of my anger, I commented things like "*You dad has such an ugly character*". Although it was true for all of the harm he had caused, these comments were damaging for my children. If you are going through a similar situation, I warn you about making these kinds of remarks, even though you have a right to express yourself in that way, due to the abuse you have suffered. But for your children's sake, don't go that route for they will remember your comments. It places a burden on their thoughts and emotions that will carry them through life. Besides, it's a form of emotional abuse for a parent to share with their child dissatisfaction, anger, or hurt he/she has in relation to the spouse. Remember their lives are too important for you to be sharing comments that will not edify their life and walk with God. Our job is to love, support and encourage them to become all they can become in God.

I remember when the church we were pastoring was beginning to notice inappropriate behaviors of the pastor. I was the church pianist and interpreted for him because we pastored a bilingual church. The first Sunday of July in the year 1997, as I went from playing the piano to my seat behind the pulpit, getting ready to interpret, he told the congregation that I was not going to interpret that day. But this was not so. In the past, I would speak at conferences, retreats or rallies and usually came home tired from ministering, asking him if I could rest the next morning, which was Sunday. But this time, I had not spoken at a special meeting and since he was not speaking to me, I had decided I was not going to try to help God by giving in to his character and asking forgiveness for something I had not done. I refused to take any kind of belittlement any more. God revealed to me that I did not have to continue in the same ongoing situation when it was not my fault. I sensed His still small voice share with me that I had experienced much patience in this long season, waiting for a change in his character, but he wasn't taking advantage of all the opportunities that God had given him and his time was up. I knew this might be a consequence I would have to pay, but I wouldn't know until I made a change to confront the unnecessary mental and emotional abuse that had gone on for years. So, instead of allowing God to intervene in the circumstances, my husband decided to take revenge. That Sunday morning, in front of the entire congregation, he lied by telling the church I was not going to interpret. I was "shocked" at his remark to the church. Suddenly, I heard the audible voice of the Lord say, *"He's not rejecting you. He's rejecting Me."* His attitude of separation behind the pulpit went on Sunday after Sunday. He was no longer allowing me to interpret by his side when he preached. Many of the young people and young married couples asked me why I was not interpreting anymore. They knew something was wrong and my response was, *"Ask the pastor"*. I didn't want the congregation to know there were marital problems because we were the Pastors. But he began to push me away even in public and the entire congregation began to see his ungodly behavior. He deliberately stopped me from playing the piano by putting someone else to play. One of the deacons tried speaking with him in regards to reconciliation, but he didn't accept anyone's advise for restoring the marriage. Pride is harmful in one's life and only causes destruction. I began to take a new seat in the pews and within three months, I was sitting in the last row until the church board asked for him to be removed as pastor.

These cruel experiences because of his action toward me are part of my past, but I will not allow it to be part of my future. I had to make a decision to remind myself of my choice for change every time the enemy wants to creep up with his darts of discouragement. It's not going to help you move forward if you're looking in the rear view mirror. Begin to walk towards your destiny, declaring what God has said, speaking His Words of life. Because His Word is life, those words that you speak allow life itself to be manifested according to His precious will and plan for peace and abundance for your life.

Recover Your "Portion"

"*How can I recover my blessings with a double portion?*" you might ask. David is a good biblical example of someone who recovered all, because he was determined to receive the blessings of his destiny. The enemy had attacked his town, taking the wives and children captive. In his despair he chose to seek his God.

In *I Sam. 30:8* we read:

> **"And David inquired of the Lord saying, Shall I pursue after this troop? Shall I overtake them? And he answered him, Pursue; for you will surely overtake them, and without fail recover all."**

"*Pursue*" means to follow in order to overtake or capture. There are several ways to pursue in order to recover those things that we have lost or things that have been taken from us. The process of a Godly, holy, and divine pursuit reminds me of the four R's (*Recover, Restore, Replenish and Rejoice*).

1. *Recover*

"*Recover*" means to get something back that was stolen. I believe this can be done by a victorious talk and a victorious walk. A victorious talk consists of words of faith of a "*worshipper*" and a spiritual *"warrior"*. These words of faith proclaim, *"The Lord is my strength. I go in the name of the Lord and in the power of His might. The Lord will never leave me nor forsake me"*. A believer with a victorious walk is one who demonstrates the walk of a *"worshipper and warrior"*. A believer with a victorious talk says, *"I walk in submission unto God and obey His Word, seeking God, and trusting Him to keep His promises"*. This committed believer will worship and war in the spirit on a daily basis until the victory is won. Though it tarries, it will come to pass, because the words of worship and faith are ready to be expressed from our mouth to the environment, in order for there to be a shift in our circumstances.

2. *Restore*

"Restore" means to return to a former state or position. The words of a believer with a victorious talk express boldness that comes from the *"worshipper and warrior"* who says, *"What is mine is coming back and I thank God for it in advance. My health is restored. My peace is restored. My finances are restored. My joy is restored. My family is restored in Jesus' name."* A believer with a victorious walk demonstrates the walk of mercy, love and forgiveness. The word *"forget"* involves a voluntary effort to not focus on something or someone. When we forgive and forget, we give the entire situation to God and do not recall or rehearse it in our mind or heart. Although it's a healing that is progressive, God is able to bring complete healing and make us whole.

3. *Replenish*

"Replenish" means to make full or complete again. The words of a believer with a victorious talk is the talk of a *"worshipper and warrior"* who says, *"He who began a good work in me shall complete it"*. The believer that demonstrates a victorious walk will be that of a dedicated *"worshipper and*

warrior" who says *"I will serve you wholeheartedly. I will live a committed, faithful walk until God replenishes me with my inheritance.* This believer will serve God, regardless of the circumstances and keep his/her eyes on the Lord until God has fulfilled His promises.

4. *Rejoice*

"Rejoice" means to be happy or glad. The victorious talk of one who rejoices is the talk of a *"worshipper and warrior"* that says, *"Rejoice in the Lord always and again I say rejoice."* The walk of a believer who is demonstrating the victorious lifestyle is the *"worshipper and warrior"* who says *"Greater is He that is in me".* It's time to get up and pursue your blessings of destiny and when obstacles come your way, take the necessary steps to remove those obstacles and keep moving forward in the name of the Lord and in the power of His Spirit.

Obstacles that will prolong the process of recuperating your blessings

Disobedience definitely prolongs the blessings. It is to your advantage to obey His commandments and be blessed.

1. Don't pursue in *"Reverse".*

"Reverse" means to turn backward or contrary to the way you are attempting to go. Defeated talk says, *"My possessions have been taken from me. I'll never get them back."* Words are very powerful and whenever we speak defeat, we get defeat. Discipline is required to speak God's Word and get God's results according to our words of faith.

2. Don't pursue with *"Rebellion"*.

"Rebellion" means to go against authority. Defeated talk says *"I'm not going to the pastor. What does he know?"* The Bible says that rebellion is like witchcraft and the longer one allows rebellion to reign, the longer our freedom to become all that God wants us to become will take place.

3. Don't pursue in *"Rejection"*.

"Rejection" means to refuse to agree with someone else. People reject others because they think they're right according to their perception, but in fact they are usually wrong. Defeated talk says *"I think my plan is better. That plan isn't going to work."* One must continuously evaluate his/her own heart and reflect on whether the Lord is sitting on the throne of one's heart.

4. Don't pursue with *"Revenge"*.

"Revenge" means to take vengeance, to inflict harm in return. Defeated talk says *"Wait till I do the same to them."* Satan enjoys it when you settle for less than the abundant life God has promised you. God says to bless our enemies and pray for them that harm you.

Recuperating your Inheritance comes with New Opportunities

God will not leave you alone through your journey from your dreams to your destiny. He knows that the enemy will try to destroy you any way he can, but remember; you are so precious before God's sight. He understands everything you've gone through; your every thought, your every pain, your every heartache. He has watched your tears stream down your face and has heard your cries. When you begin your new destiny, the true *"you"* will begin to evolve from within. Although the enemy interfered with one season in your life, God is able to *"redeem the times".* You will train your new thought life to think about a life of victory. You'll begin to say to yourself, *"Where's the next giant?" I handled it the first time with God's help and now I'm going to minister to others who are facing their giant!* Victory is ahead because His Spirit takes you daily towards your destiny.

During the years between 1997 through the present, I had to wait upon the Lord to open new doors of opportunity in regards to ministry. I continue to work in the educational field as the Coordinator of the English Learners Program in the school district where I am employed, but I had to wait until the Lord gave me a fresh beginning in ministry. God sees your faithfulness when you participate in His service in the church and in due time, God promotes us, giving us greater responsibilities as the gifts develop. I had gone through multiple experiences of service in the church through my youth and college years. Before I became a pastor's wife, I had served as a missionary teacher in Bangladesh and Guatemala. When I became a Pastor's wife, I had the privilege to teach and speak in retreats, conferences and conventions. I thought we had a good future in the ministry together because God was blessing and the church was growing. But it takes a leader, dedicated to a life of consecration and prayer in order to follow God's way and not one's own.

After the investigative interview by the denomination, we, the pastoral family, had to leave the church and all of the privileges held by our positions. This was a very devastating experience for both my sons and me, since we were the victims and not the cause. For the next several years, my sons and I attended a church where we could receive the Word of healing for our souls. During that time I continued to minister alongside my mother who is an ordained minister. We ministered as a mother-daughter team and God has used our lives to touch the lives of others. God has used my mom to open windows of opportunity for me to share the Word in conferences and retreats for women. Although I was experiencing the process of healing, I was still in much pain emotionally. God gave me the strength to minister to women experiencing problems of rejection and oppression in their marriage. Although time has been a great healing factor, I recognize that my victorious talk and walk is what enabled me to press forward towards my future filled with blessings beyond measure.

Here are some wonderful scriptures for you to meditate on your inheritance:

Deut. 30:16 says:

> *"For I command you today to love the Lord your God, to walk in his ways, and to keep his commands, decrees and laws; then you will live and increase, and the Lord your God will bless you…"*

Deut. 30:2-3 declares:

> *"… When you and your children return to the Lord your God and obey him with all your heart and with all your soul according to everything I command you today, then the Lord your God will restore your fortunes…"*

Ps. 115:14 states:

> *"The Lord shall increase you more and more, you and your children."*

"Multiplication" means abundance, plenty, and increase. Your inheritance may come through your children, the next generation. Even though your circumstances in the natural are different than what the Word of God says, don't get discouraged. Keep declaring the Word every day until that powerful Word of God manifests and you recuperate your inheritance. In my case, the circumstances in the natural looked quite dim. I couldn't believe how the father of my children paid only a minimum as ordered by the court. I had to support them primarily by myself and provide financial support for college and flight school. But, God has provided for our every need and will continue to do so. To God be the honor and glory! For those of you that are not receiving the financial resources because your husband is not fulfilling his responsibility according to God's plan, I have this scripture.

I Tim. 5:8...

> *"But if any provide not for his own, and especially for those of his own house, he hath denied the faith, and is worse than an infidel."*

So, continue to read and reread the above scriptures until they take form in your spirit with an abundance of faith. Whatever is in the heart will be expressed in your talk. So speak words of faith, because faith moves the hand of God to place you in the position that will bring you favor.

A Woman of Faith Inherits her Portion

There is a beautiful story in the Bible found in **II Kings 4:8-23**. This is a wonderful testimony of how a woman of faith pursued her portion, regardless of her circumstances. This woman is known as the Shunammite woman. The Bible tells us that she had no children, but sowed seed into the life of the prophet Elisha, by providing accommodations for him to stay in her home. When he found out that she was barren, he prophesied that she would bear a son the following year. And so it was that she gave birth to a son. Several years had passed and one day her young son became ill and died. This Shunammite woman carried her son who was dead and laid him on the bed of the prophet. She sought out the prophet to come to her house to pray for her son, restoring to her, her "*portion*" or inheritance. If you carefully read the scriptures, she never said that her son was dead, indicating that her hope was in the promises of the covenant. Anticipating an answer of "*life*" for her circumstances, the splendor of God was manifested in her life, permitting her inheritance and portion of destiny to be restored. We have to be careful to choose our words, making sure they are words of life for our circumstances. Our words determine which dreams live or die. Anticipate His resurrection power in you, declaring life into your circumstances, calling forth life to your destiny and watching the splendor of His majesty be manifested by His glory and His presence. No one can call life into your circumstances but you. Others can pray and make declarations over your life, but you have to believe and be in agreement or nothing will happen. At least, there will be delays, because it's all about your faith in the One who is able to do the miraculous.

- *Faith is seeing the invisible.*

- *Faith is believing the incredible.*

- *Faith is doing the impossible.*

There are four specific instructions for taking God's Word for your needs.

Prov. 4:20-2 says:

> ***"My son (daughter), attend to my words; incline your ear unto my sayings. Let them not depart from your eyes; keep them in the midst of your heart. For they are life unto those that find them and health to all their flesh."***

1.   Attend to my words.
2.   Incline your ear unto my sayings.
3.   Let them not depart from your eyes.
4.   Keep them in the midst of your heart.

"Attend to my words" means God wants our undivided attention because if He's going to speak to us in regards to our destiny, we need to listen to Him with our full and respectful attention. How we approach God's Word is just as important as listening to God's Word.

"Incline your ear unto my sayings" means we need to bend down and pay attention to what we are hearing.

> ***Mark 4:24*** says, ***"Take heed what you hear."***
>
> ***Luke 8:18*** states, ***"Take heed how you hear."***

What we hear is very important. We need to learn to listen with both ears, not only with one, because that causes confusion. How we hear is the key to receiving faith.

Romans 10:17 tells us:

> ***"So then faith cometh by hearing, and hearing by the
> word of God."***

When we listen to the Word of God, we develop our faith.
Many people read the Bible, but never develop the ability of
"*hearing*" the voice of God because their minds are occupied
with other things. God works in us only insofar as we receive
His Word. If we don't receive it, it doesn't work like we'd
like it to.

"***Let them not depart from your eyes***" means we must learn
to focus on God's Word. If we don't focus on His sayings,
we'll have blurred vision of spiritual things. We can't afford
to look in different directions with our eyes.

"***Keep them in the midst of your heart***" means to guard
your heart with all of your strength because everything in
life comes out of the heart as written in ***Prov. 4:23***:

> ***"Keep they heart with all diligence; for out of it are the
> issues of life."***

What you have in your heart will determine all that you
experience in your life. So God is saying that if His Words
and His sayings are kept in your heart and you apply them
in your life, they are going to do what He has promised.
They must penetrate the deepest part of your heart. So, keep
them in the central place of your whole life.

Your Mantle of Favor

Your mantle represents God's favor that is upon you due to
your covenant blessings. "*Favor*" means gracious kindness,
a token of love, endless support, opportunities of success,

promotions, and advancements because of God's love for you. Your mantle is your assignment from God with corresponding authority to fulfill it. Identify your mantle and put it on. If you don't have authority and favor, you won't receive God's full destiny for you. *"I don't know what kind of mantle I have?"* you might ask. Well, there are different kinds of mantles for life's purpose. We have mantles of favor and authority as daughters of the Most High God. These mantles represent the call on your life and that's why there is conflict, because Satan doesn't want you to recognize your calling. There are also office ministry mantles which represent the five-fold ministry callings according to *Eph. 4:11-16...*

"He gave some, apostles; and some, prophets; and some, evangelists; and some, pastors and teachers; for the perfecting of the saints...".

These callings are for full-time ministries in the Church that benefit the Body of Christ to equip, mature and bring believers into the unity of the faith. As we look at the different characters in the Bible, we see the mantles they used. Priests wore designated clothing as commanded by Levitical Law. Kings and queens dressed for their position as did military officers. Their dress represented their identity and authority. If you're a mom, you have a mothering mantle and must use it with God's authority and favor and in the lives of your children in the area of education, character training and opportunities needed to prepare them to step into their future destiny. Some mantles are to be worn all the time, but others are to be put on only when you assume the position of that mantle.[1] When I step into my assignment from God, I put on the mantle associated with my assignment. Women of God, this is not the day you are to remain hidden in closets, caves or in an identity that God never intended for you! This is a day when you are to arise, mantled with your calling and authority to carry out your calling. You are favored to become all you were destined to become!

Believe that God will make a way. Meditate on your portion, which is God's favor for your life. Don't allow favor to be stripped from you. Don't allow Satan to take your sight off your destiny. Don't meditate on your feeling of betrayal, accusation, abandonment, rejection, or guilt. Don't spend your time and energy on those things that will not change anything. Spend time thinking and meditating on the glorious plan and purpose that God has for you. Your mantle is the divine assignment from God with corresponding authority to fulfill it. *Isaiah 61:10* declares *"...He covered me with a garment of righteousness"*. You must identify your garment and then put it on. It belongs to you. Wear it! If you can't see it, you can't put it on. If you don't put it on, you won't wear it. If you don't wear it with purpose, you won't fulfill your destiny. You see, the mantle can only be placed on the one whose spirit, soul and body has been fitted for its anointing. I can assure you that if you've been washed with the blood of the Lamb, the mantle fits. It was made for you and just the right size. So wear it with joy!

In my family there has been a ministry mantle of spiritual blessings in the lives of women from generation to generation. My grandmother Lolita Flores Medina was a great woman of God, taking the Gospel and ministering to women wherever she went throughout the United States and Mexico, preaching of a loving Savior.

My mother, Delia Medina Mora, has also been used tremendously of God to reach out to women throughout most of Latin America, preaching in women's conventions as President of Women's Ministries of the Pacific Latin American District. My mom's sister, my aunt Margaret Alarcon has also been used mightily by God as President of Women's Ministries of the Hispanic Midwest District, ministering throughout the United States, Mexico and Central America. I have seen the evidence of generational blessings as the mantle has passed on from generation to generation. But, this generational blessing has not come easily. There are requirements of receiving and maintaining the mantle: a vow of total surrender and giving your life to serve Him wholeheartedly. Although generations have passed, each one of us has faced hindrances to carry the mantle; hindrances of fear, injustices, anxiety, criticism, and tragedies. But with every divine privilege, there's a divine responsibility. With every honor, there's a discipline involved. With recognition, there's a sacrifice to be made. With a walk of surrender and obedience comes the anointing to wear your mantle to fulfill your destiny. It's time to take the necessary steps to recuperate your inheritance by allowing Jesus to be your Husband. Take on His nature by drawing close to Him, sharing His love with your children and others. Then you'll begin to see God's favor arise and divine connections will begin to appear before your very eyes. My favorite scripture is **Prov. 3:5-6...**

"Trust in the Lord with all thine heart and lean not unto thine own understanding. In all thy ways, acknowledge Him and He shall direct thy paths."

Move forward in all that God has for you because the best is yet to come!

1 Barbara Yoder, <u>Mantled with Authority</u>, (Colorado Springs, CO, Wagner Publications, 2003)

Chapter 6:
Your "Suddenly" Awaits You

<u>Woman of Excellence</u>

"*Suddenly*" is a surprising moment in time when a change takes place. This is a moment in time when God operates and a miracle is manifested. That miracle could be in the form of a revelation, an open door, a divine connection or an answer to prayer. At that moment in time wisdom is acquired to make a decision to walk through that open door of opportunity.

Your "*suddenly*" is waiting for you. The winds are waiting to blow on your behalf. They are just waiting for your words of faith to be released. The wind comes with a double portion for you. Believe it in your heart and spirit. God has a heavenly deposit for you for your generation.

II Tim. 1:14 tells us to:

> ***"Guard the Good deposit that was entrusted to you."***

When He saved you, He deposited salvation in your spirit. Your body is the temple of the Holy Spirit. We must keep watch and preserve your good deposit. If your heart is sincere, and you've let go or are in the process of letting go of the past, then you've got to listen to what God is saying to your heart by His Spirit. That still small voice within you is the Holy Spirit, giving you wisdom and guidance to make the right choices. Sometimes the guidance that the Spirit of God is giving doesn't seem practical or acceptable to religious society. Nevertheless, that voice of peace and comfort within encourages you to move in a particular direction. Not to say that you shouldn't seek counseling. God can speak to you through your family, friends, a counselor or your pastor. But you need spiritual discernment to recognize the voice of God and His guidance in order to know which direction to take. After receiving counseling, your first priority is to hear the voice of the Lord for a final decision. He will lead you in the way you should go.

Become All You Can Become

All of life's experiences have shaped us into the person we have become. The secret of being transformed from a vulnerable victim with hurts and scars, to a victorious, loving person, are found in the ability to trust God in your present and for your future. In the middle of what seems like confusion, there is no other way but to trust God to guide you on your new journey that will change your life, opening new doors of opportunities in your favor. You can endeavor to make the trip easier to transition if you make Jesus your new Husband. He will not lie to you, mistreat you in any way, abuse you, belittle you or betray you. He is the ultimate Husband because He loves you as you are and will compliment your life as no other will. At some point, He will reveal to you why you had to go through what you did to become what you shall become. In the meantime, continue to study His Word and learn about His covenant laws. The highest level of pleasing Him is your walk of obedience. Obedience gives you the right to release your faith for the promises God has declared in His Word.

When you look in the mirror, speak these declarations:

- ***I have been set apart for God's purpose.***
- ***I am His chosen generation, His royal priesthood***
- ***I am the Bride of Christ***

You are anointed with the ability and capacity to fulfill your destiny, to rule for ministry and service in and out of the home, in the marketplace and wherever God takes you. Barbara Yoder shares in her book, <u>Mantled with Authority</u>, that God has given us a mandate, which is an assignment entrusted by Him who sets us apart from others and for which we are sent out to accomplish. He will anoint us with fresh oil so that we can accomplish the mandate with great joy. God is taking off the veils that have hidden women's true calling and destiny. This is a new day of unveiling and releasing. God is uncovering and releasing the seed of destiny within every person. This is going to result in an increasing measure of anointing in the home, marketplace, government, schools, churches and businesses where God has assigned us. For this to take place, you will need to be committed to God's mandate. It's going to take commitment to your God given mandate and destiny.

Be committed with the following:

1. <u>Committed to the knowledge of His Word</u>

> ***II Pet. 1:3-4*** states, ***"His divine power has given us everything we need for life and godliness through our knowledge of him who called us by his own glory and goodness. Through these he has given us his very great***

and precious promises, so that through them you may participate in the divine nature..."

God wants you to be knowledgeable in the spiritual realm and the natural realm. God has so much for you, but you can't take hold of the greater things God has to offer unless you have the knowledge of what He has provided for you.

2. <u>Committed to fulfill His Plans</u>

Prov. 16:9 says, *"We should make plans...counting on God to direct us."*

Prepare yourself for how God will be your total guide for the future. He will unlock your significance, security and success. Your steps are ordered of the Lord, so walk in His ordered steps.

3. <u>Committed to Wisdom</u>

Prov. 2:7-8 declares *"He holds victory in store for the upright; he is a shield to those whose walk is blameless, for he guards the course of the just and protects the way of his faithful ones."*

God encourages us to ask for wisdom as stated in the book of James. Therefore, you have wisdom available to you. So, trust God to give you the wisdom you need during this season in your life.

4. <u>Committed to Faith</u>

James 1:25 explains, *"But the man (woman) who looks intently into the perfect law that gives freedom, and continues to do this, not forgetting what he(she) has heard, but doing it – he (she) will be blessed in what he (she) does."*

You need to visualize yourself in victory. See yourself where God wants you to be. That's what faith is, believing your position exists and allowing the Holy Spirit to guide your steps to take your territory.

As you become a woman of excellence, you will fulfill your purpose in the Kingdom. In life, you will move from one purpose to another; from one glory to another. When you die to yourself, you allow the queen to arise. Before you can excel, you need to know (acknowledge, declare, perceive, discern) that you have been "*set apart*" as stated in ***Ps. 4:3***.

> *"**Know that the Lord has set apart the godly for himself...**"*

God knew you before the foundation of the earth and sanctified you even before you came into this world according to ***Jer. 1:5***...

> *"**Before I formed you in the womb I know you, before you were born I set you apart; I appointed you as a prophet to the nations.**"*

When Jesus was in the wilderness, He came out powerful in the Spirit because He invaded Satan with His righteousness. Righteousness simply means to be in the right standing with God. There are various levels of power (position) of righteousness; just like there are various levels of the power of the Spirit. No one has more Holy Spirit than another: but differences in power. ***Eph. 3:20*** tells us:

> *"**Now to him who is able to do immeasurably more than all we ask or imagine, according to his power that is at work within us.**"*

Compromise is not an option. The power of righteousness will bring you victory. It will make you more than a conqueror. It will assure you of your promise. Your mission in life is like crossing the sea. You'll find the smiling sunshine, clear blue sky, calm waters, favorable breezes, dark clouds, storms, angry waves and rough adverse winds. Remember that Jesus Christ is the source, the course, and the force to reach your destiny.

Ps. 37:23-24 tells us:

> *"If the Lord delights in a man's (woman's) way, he makes his (her) steps firm, though he (she) stumble, he (she) will not fall, for the Lord upholds him (her) with his hand."*

You can be in any of these positions, walking forward, backward, or be at a standstill. Your walk depends on your talk and your talk depends on your hearing. So, listen up and allow God to speak to you because He wants to make up for the lost time. God's getting you lined up for the right position at the right time. God is going before you, making the crooked places straight. He's working on getting your connections ready for you that will open doors you can't imagine.

God spoke to me recently through a pastor who came to visit my church. During the preaching, he ministered to four people through a prophetic word. I was one of those four persons. He didn't know me and I had never seen him before. He told me, *"You've had many losses, but God is going to restore all of those losses back to you and your sons."* If that prophetic word is true, it will come to pass in God's time. I just continue to trust God as my Provider.

As my Guide, I have to believe God to provide for everything in my future, including relationships. If you're thinking about future relationships as far as marriage is concerned, those ideas and thoughts need to be taken to God. Remember that all godly relationships, ones that are biblical and balanced, thrive on mutual submission, honor, respect, dignity, love and commitment to each other in Christ. The key word is *"mutual"*, which means *"reciprocal, having the same relation one for the other."* If you're afraid to trust in someone again, it's because you gave yourself unreservedly to the one that betrayed you. This is a natural reaction to feel cautious, but you also have to watch for defensiveness, which is the reaction of somebody who has been hurt once too often. In this case, the one who suffers is you. In the book of Isaiah we find a picture of betrayal when the Lord was comforting His people Israel through the prophet Isaiah. He compared them to a wife who has been rejected by her husband.

> *"Do not be afraid; you will not suffer shame. Do not fear disgrace; you will not be humiliated. You will forget the shame of your youth and remember no more reproach of your widowhood. For your Maker is your husband, the Lord Almighty is his name, the Holy One of Israel is your Redeemer; his is called the God of all the earth. The Lord will call you back as if you were a wife, deserted and distressed in spirit, a wife who married young, only to be rejected," says your God.*

> *Isa. 54:4-6*

Women that are single again ask themselves, *"Am I afraid to trust because I'm afraid to be let down or betrayed again?"* We wonder whether any of these issues are still affecting our lives. If this is you, I encourage you to continue to take your life to God on a daily basis and surrender to His will. The more you surrender, the more you find that you have new things to surrender. But He will bring healing and in turn, you will bring healing to others. God will work wonders in our lives so in turn; we can be a blessing to others.

The enemy has tried to chain us to the circumstances of the past, keeping us from reaching our potential as women of God. But he is defeated and cannot fulfill his plan if we don't allow him to. If your ability to connect emotionally with others is difficult because of your past experiences, ask God to direct you to safe, attaching, forgiving people. You need to look back and thank God for how He has kept you through life's struggles. We all need stewardship over how we conduct our lives. Remember, we are responsible for ourselves, bearing our burdens, but only partially responsible for the normal burdens of others as we choose to help them get through their storms in life. We will hurt ourselves and others if we take the wrong burden again. We do not want to go down that route. We've come too far moving towards our destiny to take another detour or delay. We already had to pay a great price for the decisions of others. Allow God to bring someone into your life according to His will. Take the time to evaluate the person's character and look for qualities of sincerity, generosity, and a passion for God. God's will, even in that area of your life, is at your disposal. You have free access to seek the Lord for His will and desire for your life. Celebrate who you have become through the assistance and power of the Spirit of the Most High God.

Destined to Dream

Recognize your God-given calling. Others might not recognize it, but remember it doesn't matter whether they recognize it or not. You know your calling and so does God!

You are called and commissioned to be:

1. *A Courageous Warrior*

2. *An Obedient and a much loved Daughter of the Most High God*

3. *A Faithful Servant*

4. *A Co-Heir with Christ*

5. *A Joint Intercessor in Heavenly Places*

You are called to your full inheritance in Christ:

1. *Called into your full gifts and talents to any office to which the Lord has or may grant to you in the future.*

2. *Called into the manifest generational blessings bestowed upon you through your family line.*

3. *Called into a wise and full use of all of your God-given resources – physical, emotional and spiritual.*

Place your name in the following declaration entitled *"I am Blessed!"*

I, _____, will be faithful to obey all the Lord my God tells me to do in His Word. He will bless and honor me more than I can imagine. All of the following blessings will gently settle on me. I will be blessed no matter where He assigns me to live. My children will be a blessing and be blessed. All of my labor will be profitable. No matter where I go, I will be blessed! The Lord will cause my enemies to fail in their plans. The Lord will summon a blessing on my financial account and on all that I attempt to do. He will bless me in the home He gave me, with divine health and wisdom. He will transform me and set me apart as His, if I do what He instructs me to do. The people around me will notice that I am special to the Lord and will be in awe. The Lord will give me abundance of prosperity: children, material goods, production in my occupation and ministry. God will assign His angels to bestow His blessings upon me. The Lord will open His storehouse so that I will have all that I need to do His will for my life when I need it. He will bless all the work that I do. I will have money to lend and invest. I will always be on top, never at the bottom, if I obey the instructions of the Lord my God and never swerve from them.

These declarations are found in ***Deut. 28:1-14.***

Remember, you were set apart for God. Don't ever think your purpose is less special because it's not in the spotlight. Some women have been called to the pulpit ministry, but we are all needed in the position that He has ordained to fulfill His purpose for the salvation of souls.

Psalms 57:2 states that ***"He performs all things for you."***

Because He formed you, sanctified you, ordained you, set you apart, and performed all things for you, I encourage you to commit your life totally to Him. Don't be confused or conformed. God has greater things in store for you that you cannot even begin to imagine.

Move in what God has prepared for you

Those that aren't willing to pay the price of obedience, involvement and maturity, will never be prepared for what God has for them. Move in your anointing and in your ministry with authority. Don't allow the spirit of inadequacy, insufficiency or failure to hold you back from what God has for you. As you allow God to teach you that you are the "*apple of His eyes*", your shadow will touch people around you in a supernatural way. Where there's vision, there's provision.

The following three simple phrases are easier said than done, but I encourage you to begin your new path of deliverance and freedom by making your decision today by:

- *Removing the past*
- *Possessing the promises*
- *Walking in your destiny*

Even though the promise land seems so far off and fear sets in due to bad reports, be assured that God's covenant is in full operation. The key to success towards your destiny is your obedience. A chain of events produces the "*abundant life*": Know Him, Obey Him, and be blessed! When we pray and read His Word, we begin to know Him. When we know Him, we begin to hear His voice and obey Him. When we obey Him, we inherit the covenant blessings of God. No matter where you've been, there is a mandate, a seed, a mantle and the power of God present to break you through to the next place. Get ready to dream like you've never dreamed before!

> *"...Write the vision and make it plain upon tables, that he/she may run that readeth it." (Hab. 2:2)*

Now is the time, woman of God, for you to understand your invaluable worth. Come into the alignment God has for you and exercise the unique gifts and calling the Lord has for you at this strategic time in history. Yes, it'll take some time, but be patient and enjoy the journey because God's Word states in *Hab. 2:3*...

> *"For the vision is yet for an appointed time, but at the end it shall speak, and not lie: hough it tarry, wait for it; because it will surely come, it will not tarry."*

When the time of fulfillment of your dream comes to pass, God will give you divine favor with others just like He gave favor to Joseph, Esther, Daniel and other ordinary men and women in the Bible. They were ordinary people with an extraordinary God. The difference was that they stayed focused on their assignment from God and trusted Him no matter the circumstances. The hand of God is upon you the same way that it was upon them. God will never birth a dream within you that is achievable without Him. Success is in Your Mouth!

Deuteronomy 30:11-14 tells us:

> *"For this commandment which I command you this day is not too difficult for you, nor is it far off. (It is not a secret laid up) in Heaven, that you should say, 'Who shall go up for us to Heaven and bring it to us, that we may hear and do it?' Neither is it beyond the sea, that you should say, 'Who shall go over the sea for us and bring it to us, that we may hear and do it?' But the word is very near you, in your mouth, and in your mind and in your heart, so that you can do it" (AMP).*

God wants us to decree His Word to release favor, breakthrough, and victory. He will place us in a strategic alignment in order to reach our prosperity. When we decide the past is over, and it is time to step into a new day, in a new way, God's light will shine brightly on the new path. By faith, you can succeed in crossing over into a new dimension of success!

So, arise to your destiny! Begin to dream again and dare to reach your destiny in God!

Most of the following questions were taken from the book, <u>Secrets of Your Family Tree,</u> by the following authors (Carder, Henslin, Townsend, Cloud & Brawand). They have allowed me to reflect on my immediate family, my own experiences and behaviors to help me have a better understanding of my original family. God created the institution of family and desires that each family have access to the blessings of God's covenant. The obedience of one person in the family can begin to open doors of opportunities in order to receive these blessings of God.

Questions of Reflection

1. Time by itself does not heal wounds. What issues have you put off, hoping that time would change them? Reflect on those issues or events in your family that you do not want to face.

2. What relationships have you been avoiding taking steps to improve?

3. What kind of inappropriate relationships exist in your immediate family history (grandparents, parents)? Who was inappropriately close? What impact have these relationships had on you, your relationship to your spouse and your relationship with God?

4. Who is most frequently blamed for family problems (black sheep)?

5. Who is/was the "*problem*" in the family?

6. Who is/was angry, mean and/or controlling in your family?

7. Which parent had the most power in your family? How did he-she use it? How did that parent maintain power and keep everybody in line?

8. Are there occasions when some of the member of your family "*don't talk to each other*" for indefinite periods of time?

9. Are your children carrying unhealthy relationship styles into their dating/marital relationships?

10. How did/does the particular religious views of your church impact your family? Did those views keep your family from changing? What has been difficult for you to change in your current family as a result of your religious training?

11. What one individual seems to have the most influence in your relationships? Why? Is it appropriate for that individual to have that much influence?

12. Do you want to withdraw from friends and family when you feel hurt or when you've done something wrong?

13. Are you too quick to criticize and/or judge others?

14. Do you become defensive quickly whenever someone asks you a question and/or tries to offer constructive feedback?

15. How can the past have such a hold on the present and the future? If "*all things are made new in Christ Jesus*", why won't "*forgetting the past*" heal the pain with its consequences?

16. How might woundedness and shame in one's background affect his/her present life and ministry?

17. Are you afraid to trust in someone because you expect to be let down betrayed, attacked or made to feel guilty again?

18. Do you have difficulty respecting others' boundaries and/or hearing their needs?

19. Can I commit to forgiving?

20. What is my greatest fear about setting limits with others?

21. What are some actions steps you might take now in order to begin to move forward with your destiny?

Scriptures of Destiny

*He is my Provider	*Renewing my Mind	* Belief & Faith in my God
Deut. 28:11-13	Isa. 26:3	II Cor. 4:8-9
Phil. 4:19	Rom. 12:2	Ps. 138:7
II Cor. 9:6-8	II Cor. 10:5	John 14:1
Luke 6:38	Col. 3:2	Rom. 8:28
III John 2	Rom. 8:6-8	Ps. 121:1-2
*Jesus, My Companion	* Guidelines for Growth	*He is my Peace
John 15:15-16	Matt. 22:36-39	Isa. 26:3
James 4:8	Rom. 12:2	Phil. 4:6-7
Isa. 54:10	II Tim. 2:15	Isa. 26:12
John 14:18	II Tim. 1:7	Ps. 119:165
Ps. 27:10	Gal. 5:22-23	Isa. 57:2
*My Trust in Him	* My Obedience to Him	* His Amazing Love for Me
Prov. 3:5-6	Matt. 21:28-32	John 14:219-10
Isa. 26:4	Luke 6:46-49	Jer. 31:3
Nah. 1:7	Isa. 30:21	Prov. 8:17
Deut. 7:9	Phil. 4:13	I John 4:10-12
II Thess. 3:3	Heb. 5:8	John 15:10
*He is Forever Faithful	*Favors and Blessings for Me	* Rejoice in your Inheritance
I Thess. 5:24	Ps. 84:11	Ps. 5:11
Rom. 4:20-21	Prov. 8:35	Isa. 54:13
Isa. 46:10-11	Isa. 61:7	Acts 2:39
II Pet. 3:9	Jer. 29:11	Joel 2:28
Isa. 59:1	Ps. 5:12	I Pet. 1:4
*His Divine Promises	*Deliverance from evil	*God's Chosen Vessel
Mark 11:24	Isa. 41:10	Isa. 44:21
Isa. 65:24	Ps. 34:4	Ps. 4:3
Deut. 7:11-13	Isa. 35:4	Ex. 19:5-6
John 15:7	Isa. 43:1-3	Col. 1:11-12
Ps. 91:14-16	Ps. 56:13	John 15:16